NO LOVE

A True Story

Sometimes, the monsters are the ones that are supposed to

love you

Printed in the United States of America

First Printing, 2018

For information and permission contact;

Josephclarke21@yahoo.com

Cover Illustration by Nicole Suazo©2018

NO LOVE

By JOSEPH J. CLARKE

INTRODUCTION

I was born on March 17, 1983, in Frontier, Port Maria Saint Mary Jamaica W.I. I discovered my love for writing in the ninth grade and all props go to my ninth-grade science teacher, Mr. Flex. Mr. Flex's class was challenging, but I enjoyed all 60 minutes of that class. He was one those of teachers who had bad penmanship on the chalkboard, and if you didn't keep up you would be lost because he hated repeating himself. What I enjoyed about his class was how he would read aloud to the class. While most of the class hated this method, I loved it. I would pay close attention to what he was saying so I could tune out everything that was going in my life at the time. I was free from all hurt during that hour. That ninth-grade science class was my only escape from the life I had. I endured much as a child. I experienced things that no child in the world should ever have to suffer. I was abused sexually at the age of seven. When I tried to tell the person who I considered my protector, I was beaten and called a liar. That day was the end of any hope for a normal childhood.

I'd kept the truth hidden due to the fear of pain that was all too familiar. I also didn't think anyone cared. It became easy for me to pretend I wasn't hurting. As I grew older, it was almost impossible for me to form bonds with anything or anyone. I didn't tell anyone about my abuse because I felt no one would ever believe the story I am about to describe. When I was seven years old, my mother left me. Though her reasons were logical, I felt neglected, rejected, and abandoned. I carried these feelings into my adult life which would later inhibit me from having successful relationships of any kind. I loved people who I thought loved me, but instead, I was hurt repeatedly. I entered every relationship keeping secrets and pushing everyone away. There was one point in my adult life when I thought I found the perfect person; the one with whom I could finally be vulnerable. However, due to my troubled past and bad decisions, I didn't open up at the right time. I was running from my past using parties and girls to hide my pain. I met this young lady broken; my lifestyle was a mess. I wanted to be perfect for her because she seemed perfect for me. For four years I was happy; I tried to keep my previous life a secret, and one day on the 4th of July my secrets caused us to separate. I experienced the worst heartbreak in my adult life. I didn't know how to handle the pain. I couldn't eat or sleep because of the breakup. The pain was reminiscent of the way I felt when my mother left me, and I became a victim of abuse. I didn't know what love was during the relationship, but I wanted to learn. I falsely believed my ex-girlfriend was the only person I that understood and loved me back. As broken as I was I gave her everything, and she never appreciated me. Whatever she needed for whatever reason I gave to her. I wanted to love her the way the men who dated my mother should have loved her. I wanted to be the man my father should have been for my mother. I wanted to love and protect our children the way I was supposed to be loved and protected. The pain got so real that it felt like my heart stopped.

A few months later I met a young lady with a beautiful spirit and the heart of a child. It was as though she had never been through any significant pain in her life. She was almost perfect. One Sunday night we were having a conversation about life. I was pouring my heart out to her about my past, and she said, "Joseph, why don't you write a book? There are a lot of people in this world hurting like you are." She continued, "some people are unable to cope and process this kind of hurt, and your writing and opening up to the world may help you and them." She spoke right through me. I heard every word she said, and I just began writing immediately. I looked around my apartment for a pen and couldn't find one, so I took out my phone and started pouring out my heart — the dysfunctional things I'd witnessed and been through and endured. I wrote every day. I walked around with a pen, and whenever I had a memory or a flashback, I would write. I was able to write this book in four weeks. Everything just came rushing back to me.

There were times I had to stop and call someone, to try and have a regular conversation so that I could ease my mind of the hurt from the memories of my past. Some nights I went to bed crying, and no matter how much I wiped the tears away they kept coming. I kept remembering how weak I was and how I was unable to help my mother. I failed to help my sister. I was unable to help myself. I was completely helpless.

I wrote this book for the truth; to help it come out of wherever it is hiding, in whoever is holding it in. I didn't tell my mother about my abuse until I was twenty-five years old, and even as an adult, I was still afraid. I didn't apologize to my sister for not being able, to tell the truth after watching her get raped by the same person who abused me. I cannot say there is a sure way of protecting your child from every harm that may come their way, but I know that there's evil everywhere, even in the people we love and trust with our children. We must keep our eyes open no matter what the circumstances may be. It is our first job as parents to love and protect our children with every fiber of our being and remember that kids are always watching — everything we do affects them, good or bad.

One day while playing soccer, someone told me that I was the angriest Jamaican they knew. A coworker also said that they have yet to meet anyone as mean as me. I'd never put much thought into those comments until recently. How did this happen? I wore my emotions on my sleeves. I tried to fit in and be normal, but it just didn't happen. I managed to lose everyone and everything I ever cared for and loved. I asked myself how I managed to love people who could walk out of my life without a second thought. I realized that I am a hurting man and loving me is probably one of the hardest things for others to do.

Writing this book is my therapy. It feels like I am sitting on the couch of a psychiatrist pouring out my heart. I decided not to emulate other books because my life experiences were not ordinary. I opened up to the people that knew me and wondered why I was so angry and mean. I am also sharing my story with the world. When I decided to write this book I had a conversation with my mother. I told her I remembered what had happened to her when I was four-years-old. She could not believe it. She went silent for a while and then she started to cry. I told her not to cry because everything was okay. She went to my grandmother and asked her about my abuse, and she denied it happened. I told my mother that I expected her to deny it, and how I figured she wouldn't admit the truth. I also said to her that my uncle, her brother, would deny everything if ever she was to see him and confront him as well.

This book is a conversation I am sharing with the hope that it may open your eyes to what can and may happen to the ones we love by the people we trust. I hope that this book can also help someone to open up about their abuse because it can eat at you; turning you bitter and hard to love. Hopefully, this will open your eyes as a parent to pay close attention to your children and grandchildren because living through this can be unbearable and the pain never stops.

THE BREAK UP

It all started in 1987. I was four-years-old, lying in bed and heard my mother screaming "STOP!!!" Yelling for help. I heard my father's voice say, "you can't tell me that!" I ran to her room and saw my father forcing himself on my mother. Although I was terrified of my father, I yelled at him and told him to get off my mom. He turned to me and said, "you should go back to bed before I whoop your ass." I went back to bed crying. I wanted to help my mother, but I was scared of my father. The rumbling went outside of the house, and the noise continued for a while, then suddenly it stopped. I did not hear my mother's voice anymore. I cried myself to sleep in fear for my mother. The following morning, I remembered waking up and rushing to my mother's bedroom to see if she was ok, but she wasn't there. I went to get my then two-year-old brother. I remembered the way to my grandmother's house, so we held hands, and walked to her house.

Sometime later I saw my mother coming, and we ran to meet her. I was so happy to see her. Once I approached her I looked in her face; tears filled her eyes and bandages were all over her face. I will never forget what she said to me, "your father did this to me." She said, "no man is going to want me now." I later found out that I walked into the room as my father raping my mother because she was breaking up with him and he was not willing to let her go. In an attempt to keep other men from finding her attractive, he slit her face thirteen times. At the time I was too young to process the magnitude of what just happened to my mother. I did not fully understand what was going on, all I knew was that my mother was hurting and I wanted to help her. After my parents separated, we had to move because my mother could not afford the home we were living in without the help of my father.

When I was five-years-old my father came to our new house and saw my mother with another guy, and he became upset, and a fight broke out. I heard the commotion and recognized my father's voice. When I got to where they were, I saw a group of people surrounding my father trying to hit him in the head with a piece of wood. I remember running between my stepfather and my father screaming and cursing telling him not to hit my father. I said, "don't hit my f*****g father. Leave him alone." With tears running down my face I stood in front of my father as a human shield ready to take any blows thrown at him. I would turn to every side my stepfather was trying to find to hit my father until my father saw an opening and ran. My stepfather and the crowd of people chased after my father. I wanted to help my father, and so I started following behind crying, yelling, and cursing telling them to leave my father alone. My mother stopped me and said, "you need to go back inside and go to your bed. If not I'm going to whoop you for cursing." I was terrified of getting a beating, so I went inside the house. I could not sleep because all I thought about was them killing my father and not being able to see him again. I waited up and cried for my mother.

Once my mother came back I asked her if my father was ok and she told me that they couldn't catch him; I was so relieved and was finally able to sleep. I didn't see my father much after this incident. I blamed my stepfather for my father's absence. Times became hard; harder than they were before because my father stopped taking care of us and my mother was doing it all by herself. Although it was rough, my mom tried her best. There were days where I would have to go in nearby farms and eat whatever I saw available to eat; sugar canes, watermelons, coconut, and sometimes ripe bananas. I would have to be extremely careful because in Jamaica, as a way to set an example, the farmers kill anyone they catch stealing their produce. Taking food became normal for me.

MOTHER LEFT ME

About a year later Hurricane Gilbert blew through Jamaica. We had to evacuate our neighborhood, and everyone went to a school that was close by for shelter. The wind and rain were unlike anything I have ever seen. We watched our homes got destroyed by the wind and rain. My life as I knew it was never the same; everything for everyone was gone. Every area that I could see became flooded. After the storm passed everyone went to their homes to estimate the damages and see what they could salvage, but there was nothing to save.

After the storm, everyone had to stay in the shelter for a while because there were nowhere else for us to go. A group of missionaries came to the shelters to offer help and give food. They wanted to make homes for all the families affected by the storm. They were able to build temporary tents so that we could be with our families and from there they built homes for us to move into once they finished the

15

new homes. My father signed himself up for a home and somehow was fortunate enough to get the home. My mother, on the other hand, was not lucky as had to be innovative and made a house from the leftover boards. Although she did her best, it was only a one-room house for the five of us, my mother and her four children. Whenever it rained, the floor would turn into mud puddles, so we would have to stay in bed or get stones to step on so we could get outside. The factory that my mom worked for never reopened and things started to get even worse, and it seemed as if my father couldn't care less. I believe the more we suffered, the more he thought that my mother would run back to him.

I had an aunt that lived in Kingston; she had a job at the same type of factory that my mom worked at before the hurricane. One weekend my aunt came over to see about her son who was staying with my grandmother. She would come over every two weeks and give my grandmother money to take care of him. He was mute and unable to speak. My aunt told my mother about the open positions at her job, and my mother decided to apply. My mother thought it was her only option to be able to provide for us. Finding out my mother was moving to Kingston was the third time I had my heart broken into pieces. I felt I would rather not eat and not have clothing than to be without my mother; she was all I knew.

At the age of seven, I believed it was my responsibility to protect my mother; I figured I would not be around to protect her if she moved so far away. The day my mother and aunt left I cried so hard. It felt like my chest was going to explode. I could not understand why she would leave me. I did not care about her coming back; I did not want her to leave, not for a second. I remember that Sunday like it was yesterday because that day was so painful in so many ways. I was so upset she left, and we had to stay with my grandmother who was not the kindest person.

　　After my mother was gone, my grandmother told me to stop crying or leave her place, so I stepped outside of the gates to cry. I was not facing my grandmother, and the next thing I know I was hit in the head with a rock and fell forward. I guess I wasn't far away enough for her comfort so while I was still crying she picked up a rock and threw it at me. The rock hit me in the head and busted my head open. I did not know what happened, but when I looked back I saw her looking at me, and she said, "I told you to leave my place with the noise or shut up." Despite the pain and bloody clothes I got up off the ground and ran as fast as I could. It had made me cry even harder because I felt I was right about not wanting my mother to leave. She would have never done that to me. It was only half a day since my mother left and I already had my head busted open. I took off my shirt to cover the wound on my head and walked around in the streets until nightfall. It was seven of us

staying in a one bedroom with two beds; my place was on

the floor. My living conditions had always been bad, but it

was all that I knew.

THE RAPE

Seven-years-old was the beginning of the end of a normal childhood. We had to go to the bushes miles away from our house, up in the hills to find wood to cook. On Sundays, we also had to carry water on our heads to drink, cook, and do laundry. We had to chase and kill the chickens my grandmother picked out for dinner. My uncle who lived with us came up with an idea to set a trap for the chicken because chasing it was getting hard and frustrating. He made a knot out of fishing line and put chicken feed in the middle, and when the chicken comes to eat, he will pull the knot slowly until it tightens on its feet. It made it impossible for it to get away.

One Sunday morning, my grandmother sent me, my mute cousin, and my uncle to get some wood and coconut. We had a handmade cart to fill up with the wood and coconut. I remember walking past the top of a hill where you could look down and see several trees below. As the wind blew on them, the wind would continue to the top of the hill, and even though the sun was hot, the wind would blow over the hill and give off a cool breeze. I asked my uncle, "Where are we?" and he replied, "we are at the breezy park." I was going to ask him why it called breezy park, but the look of the trees going back and forth and coolness of the wind hitting our faces explained it. We went into the woods and left the cart on the side of the road and gathered all the dry wood we could find and brought them back to the cart.

After collecting the wood, we pushed the cart to the side of the hill where the coconut trees were. My cousin and I were too little to climb the trees, so my uncle told us to stay on the slope of the hill to stop the coconuts from running down to the bottom of the hill. We caught and gathered them and took them to the cart. On our way back to my grandmother's house my uncle told me to follow him to this abandoned building to look for something. He signed to cousin to watch the cart in case someone tried to steal our coconuts. He did not tell me what we were going to do, but being that he is my uncle I trusted to follow him.

When we got inside the building, he pushed me down to the ground. I was confused and didn't know what was happening before I knew it he was on top of me and pulling my clothes off. I asked him what is he doing. He said, "Shut up, and I'll give you one of the coconuts for yourself." I said, "no, get off me!" He pulled my clothes off and forced himself inside of me. The pain was excruciating; it was unlike any other pain I had ever felt before. I started to yell out for help, but he covered my mouth.

I tried to bite his hand, but I could not. His hands were bigger than my mouth, and my teeth could not grab hold of his hand. I could not breathe. I felt like I was suffocating. I thought I was about to die. I was praying for someone to come and save me, but no one ever came. It finally ended, yet felt like it lasted a lifetime. I could not move. I stayed there on the ground in pain, and my clothes had blood on them. I felt violated, robbed, hurt and in intense pain — the worst experience I have ever had. I was so confused; all I wanted was my mother.

I cried out; my uncle told me to get up. I obeyed, and he begged me not to tell. He said, "I will give you as many coconuts as you need if you don't tell." I said, "I don't care. I am telling grandma." At seven years old I was experiencing something no one in the world should have to experience. I cried the whole way back to my grandmother's house; I could not wait to tell my grandmother what happened to me. The whole walk to her house my uncle kept begging me not to say anything to my grandmother. It was a very long walk back. As we got closer to her house, I heard shouting. It was an older man. He was yelling for us to stop. We slowed down, and he caught up to us. He had a machete in his hand. He looked at my uncle and said. "What did you do to him?" My uncle replied. "I didn't do anything to him. He's just spoiled and crying because he doesn't want to help do any of the work." I immediately replied, "that's a lie!" I started to tell the man what my uncle had done to me, but as I was explaining what happened my grandmother heard the shouting and rushed to us.

My uncle told her that I was trying to tell a lie on him. My grandmother told me to shut my mouth and go in the yard. I did as she said, but had no clue what was about to take place. I heard my uncle and the stranger yelling back and forth at each other. The man knew my uncle had done something wrong to me. He was a stranger and was trying to protect me. She asked me what happened and I told her that my uncle raped me. I said to her that he pushed me down and forced my clothes off me. Suddenly, my uncle began yelling out that I was lying and told my grandmother to ask my mute cousin, but he was on the outside watching the cart. He had no clue what happened. He could not even hear us, and so he did not listen to him begging me not to tell. At this point, it was my word against his, and he was louder and older, so I didn't get a chance to speak because he kept talking over me. My grandmother told my uncle to get a switch. I had no idea what was about to happen. My grandmother asked me why I was telling lies? I told her, "I am not lying!" She didn't believe me, so she beat me, all the while I kept yelling that I was telling the truth. It seemed like every time I told her I was telling her the truth she hit me harder.

Jamaica was very homophobic at the time, so if people found out about my rape, he would've been in serious trouble. Most likely beaten, killed, or sent to prison, but my grandmother wanted him to get away with it than for me to speak about it. She made sure I never repeated it by making me fear her or rather worry about getting another beating. After the whipping was over, I had bruises all over my body. I ran outside on the street and cried out for my mother. I needed her right then and there more than anything in the world. I needed someone or something to protect me from the monsters around me. The people who were supposed to love and protect me were the ones abusing me mentally, physically, emotionally, and sexually. I could not sleep that night. I stayed up all night on the floor, asking God to help me. The following morning, I woke up before everyone and sat outside under a tree. I was hurt and saddened by what happened the day before, and I was still in pain and shocked from the sexual assault and beating I got for being honest. I got raped and beaten to keep quiet on the same day.

The next morning, I went walking down the street and found some empty paint containers. I brought them back home and started to play with them. I would stack them up on each other and imagine that they were a huge wall that I built to protect me from everyone around. I wished no one could touch me, or no one could ever get inside to hurt me again. I was outside playing for a while, and eventually, my cousins woke up. They all came running out and one of my older cousins, who tends to bully me because of our age difference, spotted the containers. He decided that he wanted to play with them also, so he tried to take them away. I wasn't in the mood for the bullying, so I asked him to leave me alone. He knocked over my containers. Out of anger, I cried and re-stacked them. Once again, he whacked them back down. At this point I was furious. He had knocked them down three times, picked up one of the containers and repeatedly beat him with it. I was in a rage, so it was hard for me to stop; there was blood everywhere.

His sisters ran over yelling and pushed me away just enough for him to escape. My uncle heard the commotion from inside the house and came outside and saw what was going on. He called my grandmother out to show her what I did. She insisted that my uncle needed to take my cousin to the hospital. My grandmother called me over and once again beat me. At this point, I begin to feel that everyone was against me. I felt as if there was no happiness within me. My mom had left me, and I was always being picked on and beaten. I started seeing everyone around me as monsters.

After my cousin came from the hospital, he was unable to walk. His knees were busted open from the paint container. All I felt when I looked at him was hate. I had no compassion because I sensed no one loved me. That weekend my mother came to my grandmother's house. I was thrilled to see her. I ran up to her and hugged her legs real tight. I wanted to tell her everything, but I was afraid she would not believe me and beat me just like my grandmother did. I also felt like my grandmother was watching me to make sure I did not mention my molestation. A part of me felt like I should blame my mother for leaving me with these people even though they're family. In my mind, they were real-life monsters.

When it was time for my mother to leave and go back to work I cried and begged her to stay. She told me that she had no other choice but to go back to work because she had to make money to take care of us. I made up in my mind that I was not staying at my grandmother's anymore. As soon as my mother left, I did too. I had nowhere to go, but I kept walking. There was a pond with a chicken coop next to it that was close to my grandmother's house; I slept there that night. It was dark and scary, but it felt safer there than with my own family.

The following morning I woke up hungry. There was a sugar cane field next to the pond. I went to the area, and as quietly as possible I got three sticks of sugar cane. That was enough to stop the hunger for a while. I went back to the pond and ate them all. While I was sitting down thinking about where I would rather be and the life I wished I had, I heard a noise in the bushes behind me. I turned around to see what or who it was and low and behold it was my uncle. I later found out that someone saw me walking back to the pond and told my uncle where to find me. My uncle grabbed me and started to beat me. He asked me, "who told you to leave the house?" I tried to run, but at my age, it was not able to outrun my uncle. He beat me the entire way back to my grandmother's house.

When we got to my grandmother's house, I was bruised and had welts all over my body. The crying caused my eyes to swell; I could hardly see. My grandmother asked him where he found me, and he told her that he saw me by the pond in the bushes. She asked me, "what would I tell your mother if something was to happen to you in those bushes?" Even though she just saw the evidence of a beating that I just received from my uncle she got her whip and insisted on beating me too. I thought I was going to die. I wished I had the power to disappear. I hated everything about my life and the people in it. I could not understand why all of this was happening to me. What had I done to deserve this? Children filled the yard, yet I felt so isolated as if I was there by myself. I felt dirty and humiliated. I did not want to talk or play with anyone. I remember waking up that following morning very angry at everything and everyone. My entire world was changing, and I was living in constant fear for my safety. I did not know when or if I would get molested or beaten again. I had no one to protect me, and no one believed me; every day felt like punishment.

My chore was to fetch water from the pipe that was located about half a mile from my grandmother's house, and I had to carry the water on my head in a bucket. The weight of the bucket when it was full was way too much for me to handle at that time, but my grandmother said if I didn't carry it, then I can't eat. It took twelve trips to the pipe to fill the drum that I was supposed to fill, when I finished, I felt like someone was standing on my head; my neck and back hurt so bad.

It was time again for my mother to come and visit us. I was up early waiting for her to get to my grandmother's house. When she arrived, I made sure to follow her around everywhere she went. I saw the look on my grandmother's face when I was walking behind my mother. She gave me a look as if she was telling me to keep my mouth shut. If not then there would be hell to pay when my mother left. I remember her saying, "hey boy! Why don't you leave your mother alone?" I did not care what she said; I just needed my mother because I was hurting. When the time came for my mother to leave, my brother and I were both crying. He was so little, and so I thought he was just spoiled, but in the back of my mind, I wanted him to be quiet so that my mom could hear my cry out for help.

I wanted to ask my mother to help me, but it felt like someone was covering my mouth an I was unable to speak. My brother and I followed our mother to the bus

stop. The whole time we were crying and begging her to

stay. She kept looking back at us telling us to turn back.

She would break branches off the nearby trees and

attempted to hit us, and we would turn around and run as if

we were going back. As soon as she turned around, we

would be right back following her. We were barefoot and

in our underwear, and the sun was scorching. The asphalt

on the road was melting under our feet. It would be hell

after my mother was gone and I knew it. I did not care how

hot the sun was or how much my feet burned from the

melting asphalt. I had to let my mother see how bad it was.

We reached in town without her knowing. My brother and I

were in town half naked with tears running down our

cheeks.

When she got on the bus, my little brother snuck on

too; I watched him as he hopped on the bus. I wanted to get

on also, but I was afraid. I was too scared of the beating I would eventually receive. I watched my mother staring at me while the bus drove away. I immediately felt a cloud of sadness come rushing over me. I felt alone now because my brother made it on the bus with my mother. I started to walk back to my grandmother's, but there was this gutter that runs on the outside of our neighborhood behind my school that grabbed my attention. The channel takes the excess water off the land when it rains heavily, and fish were swimming in it all the time. I sat there and watched them swim. It felt so peaceful, and they looked as free as I wanted to be. I was sitting there for a long time observing the fish swim when all of a sudden I heard my brother's cry and my mother yelling at him.

I ran back to my grandmother's place so that my mother would not know that I followed her to the bus station. I realized that finding my brother on the bus had my mother furious. When my mother got to my grandmother's house with my brother, I overheard her saying that she had to get off the bus to bring my brother home, and that was the last bus running to Kingston for the day. She would not be able to make it back to Kingston until the next day. That was one of the happiest days of my life. It was a temporary relief of the fear that I had. Even though my bed was a couple of sheets on the floor, I had the best sleep ever.

The next day I woke up to my mother's voice. She was dressed and getting ready to leave. I stood at the door and watched her leave again. I wanted to cry, but I had to hold back my tears. She was about to go through the gate but stopped to speak to her friend. They had a conversation about work, and she told my mother about a job close by that was hiring. My mother said she would check it out before she left for Kingston. I prayed that day for my mother to get that job. I prayed the same short prayer repeatedly all day. "Lord please let mommy get the job." A few hours later, my mother came back and said she got the job and she wouldn't return to Kingston. I yelled, "Thank you, Jesus!" I did not care who heard me; I felt liberated. I figured life would go back to normal and I would not have to go through any more abuse of any kind. My mother was there. We went back to live with our mother.

One night while I was asleep I felt someone on top of me. I could not breathe. It felt like a nightmare. I woke up out of my sleep, and it was my uncle! Again, he was forcing himself inside me. I begin to yell for my mother, but he covered my mouth. I cried so hard and tried to bite his hand, but that did not work. He suddenly stopped, but I continued crying. He begged me not to tell my mother and said that if I told her, he would say to her that I was lying on him so that I could use it as an excuse to go outside. I thought everyone would believe him since he was older and believe that I was not telling the truth. I could not go back to sleep. I later found out that my mother wanted to have a few drinks with her friends, and she didn't want to leave us by ourselves, so while we were asleep, she called our uncle over to watch us, not knowing what he had done to me before. I felt like there was no escaping this life. There was no way to get away from this constant abuse. My mother came home and saw that I wasn't sleeping and asked, "Joseph why are you up?" Before I could answer, my uncle interrupted me and said, "he's just up giving trouble." He spent the night at our place as if he was trying to intimidate me, and if that was the case, it worked because I was scared the entire night.

The following morning, I took the clothes off my clothes and threw them in the bushes behind our house. I felt sad and helpless. I wanted my mother to help me without me saying a word. I wanted her to look at me and know what was going on. I started to question why all of this was happening to me. What did I do wrong to deserve this misery? What signs did I show my uncle, if any, and how can I stop him from seeing those signs? I started to become terrified of every adult I saw. It did not matter who they were. If I were alone, I would run and hide in the bushes until they passed. If I were going to the store, I would run as fast as I could and run straight back home. I did not want anyone to see me. I had no clue if I would get abused again, but I knew one place that I decided I would never go to again and that was my grandmother's house. It did not matter what was happening there; I was never going back through her gates.

SKIPPING SCHOOL

The new school year began. I was now in the first grade. I felt weird being around others after what happened during the break. I felt naked like everyone was looking at me and they all knew what happened. On the first day back, the principal walked around to each of the classes and introduced himself to everyone. When he got to my class, he stood at the front of the class introduced himself then asked, "Can anyone tell me how much four quarters add up to be? I'll give a dollar to anyone that can give me the correct answer." I was always a smart kid; there was one thing my father did not play about, and that was general knowledge. He always told me that there are things you must know, and there is no way around it, and knowing how to count change correctly was one of those things. I immediately knew the answer was a dollar, but I was so terrified of being around people that I was scared to speak.

The boy sitting beside me attempted to guess the answer, he yelled out, "seventy-five cent!" The principal told him that the answer was wrong. I whispered to him to say a dollar, and he replied, "why don't you say it?" No one else said anything. The entire class was quiet. You could hear a pin drop. Everyone was looking at each other for the answer. I could hear my heart beating in my chest, but I decided to answer the question. I said, "a dollar." The principal asked, "who said that?" The boy next to me was quick to point me out; I guess he thought what I said was wrong. The principal told me to stand up. I stood up. I had no clue what was going to happen next. He said, "lass give him a hand." The class started clapping. He took out a dollar from his wallet and gave it to me and said, "well-done son," I responded, "thank you."

My mother could not afford to give us lunch money, so she would prepare enough food at night for our lunch the next day. We lived about half a mile from the school, on lunch break, I would jump over the school walls, go home and eat lunch and then jump back over before the bell rings. This day I did not have to go home. That dollar was enough to buy lunch for the day. That day after school I went home, and my mother asked why didn't I come back for lunch, and I told her about what happened.

One day I remember going home for lunch, and the pots were empty. I was sure my mother left us lunch, so I was confused. I had to go back to school hungry. I could hear my stomach growling. That day after school I went searching for something to eat. It was impossible for me to sneak in someone's farm because everyone was out and about. I walked on the side of a hill where I thought no one had stepped on the dirt, to see if it were edible. I tasted the soil, and it tasted ok. I ate the dirt until my stomach hurt. I went to the neighborhood pipe to drink some water to see if it would make me feel better.

When my mother got home from work, I told her that there wasn't any food when I came home for lunch. She was furious because she knew that she left food for us. She asked my older sister and my older cousin if they ate the food she left and they both denied it. The next day I came home for lunch, and again the food was gone. The hunger was unbearable, just like the previous day I had to eat dirt after school. I told my mother that someone ate our lunch again. My mother asked our neighbor who they saw around our house during the day time, and they told her they saw my older cousin. She went to him to confront him on what she heard; he denied it. I knew as soon as I heard that it was my cousin, he would lie about eating the food. I knew no one was going to break into our home to eat our lunch then leave.

My mother, being as upset as she was, decided to take matters in her own hands. She prepared two different lunches for the next day and told us not to eat the one left open because she put poison in it. She hid the other one under the bed for us to eat for lunch. On the way to school the next day, it did not feel right for me to allow my cousin to eat the poisoned so I turned back and waited until my cousin arrived. I watched him open the container, and said, "stop." He was surprised to see me. He asked why I was not in school. I told him I stayed home because of the poisoned food and I was trying to save his life. I saw the hurt in his eyes; I knew he was hungry so I shared the lunch I had with him. He said that he wouldn't eat our lunch anymore. That evening my mother came home from work, she saw the poisoned food she left out was gone. I told her no one touched it and I came back and threw it out.

I was carrying so many secrets inside, so many that it began to feel normal. I was making it through school every day without friends. I felt out of place wherever I was. My favorite place to go was up in the hills to the breezy park. I would walk for miles to be there alone. It was like my escape from my messed up life. Looking down on the wind blowing the trees was a peaceful sight. There was no one in sight, and that was the only time I felt safe.

I never had trouble doing my school work; I could solve any math problem the teacher gave me. My only issue in school how uncomfortable I felt around other people; I was unable to build a bond or a friendship with any of the other students. I never wanted to be in school, so I started to think of ways for me to not to be there. One day I decided not to go to school, my mother found out and gave me a beating so hard. While beating me, she was crying saying she had it hard and doing everything to take care of my siblings and me by herself and I am taking it for granted. She had no clue what I was going through, and I was scared to tell her. I started to feel so angry and hateful and began to resent my mother. I began to blame her for leaving me and allowing my abuse.

One Sunday when I was eight-years-old, my mother left us in the care of one of my aunts. My aunt was going to a funeral and did not have time to cook so she told me to cook and feed my brother. She left chicken and rice for me to cook. I had no clue what to do, but I decided to try. I had no choice because I was hungry. We used a wood fire to cook. I had to gather the wood and start the fire. I cut up the chicken the best way I could and seasoned it. Then I put the rice on the fire. I needed cooking oil to cook the chicken, but I could not find any. I looked everywhere I thought it would be and I did not see any. I saw a container that looked like it had oil in it. I put the frying pan on the fire then put the chicken in the pot and poured what I thought was cooking oil in the frying pan. It immediately caught fire. I did not know what to do. I had no clue what was happening. I reached for a container with water in it and poured it on everything. The fire was finally out, but everything was a mess. What I thought was cooking oil turned out to be kerosene oil.

There was no food left to cook, and my brother and I stayed hungry until our aunt came home from the funeral. When she returned the first thing she saw was the mess and called me over in a stern voice. Every child in my family was afraid of this aunt. I already knew that she was going to beat me. I started to run, but she was faster than I was. She caught me and dragged me back to the house. I tried to pull away, but her grip was too tight, I could not move my arm. She grabbed a thick piece of the firewood and took my clothes off, and laid me over her knees and started to beat me. She held me in one position and beat me continuously. I felt like I was about to pass out. The beating was the lengthiest beating I can remember ever getting. She finally let me go, and I ran as fast as I could and as far away as possible while loudly crying. At eight-years-old, I did not believe anyone in my life loved me. I went to my favorite place to be away from everyone, up in the breezy park. I was there for hours just wishing I was never born and asking God to take my life. I had no one to protect me from the monsters around me.

Meanwhile, during this time alone I begin to feel my bottom burning, and I thought it would eventually stop. When I touched my bottom, there was blood on my fingers. The beating was so severe that I was unable to sit. When I got home, I was forced to eat the food I had attempted to cook. For two whole weeks after the beating from my aunt, I could not wear underwear. Cuts and bruises covered my body. When I tried to wear shorts, the shorts would get stuck on the open wounds and would be so painful to take them off. I had to walk around without underwear and unable to wear shorts. Abuse filled every area of my life, and it seemed there was no escaping it. There was no refuge. At this point in my life was the first time I ever had a grim thought about committing suicide. All I had to look forward to was the hurt that filled my past and my present.

One day it came on the news they found a body in an open field, it turned out to be the aunt who beat me. They believed that she broke up with her boyfriend, and he killed her for leaving. The killer cut her throat and sliced out her vagina. A witness saw someone resembling the boyfriend's description chasing my aunt the night of her death. The police arrested him, but because no one came forward to make an identification they had to let him go, and until this day her murder is unsolved. I did not cry at the news of her death nor did I attend her funeral.

A few days later one of my uncles saw me walking home and told me to go to the store and get him cigarettes. He poured some water on the ground and said to me that if the water dried up before I got back that he was going to beat me. Crazy right? There were a lot of people at the store when I reached it. Immediately I knew that I was going to be in trouble and I started to cry. The people at the store were trying to figure out what was wrong with me. I told them my uncle was going to beat me for taking too long with his cigarettes. The cashier felt sorry for me and had me cash out before the others. When I got back to my uncle, he was there with a tree branch in his hand. I gave him his cigarettes, and he grabbed my arm and started to beat me because the water had dried up. He hit me until he was satisfied. It felt as if everyone enjoyed taking turns abusing me. He beat me even though I had no control over the number of people that were at the store. A few months later that uncle died in his sleep, and when I heard the news, I did not cry nor attend his funeral. At nine-years-old, I had already experienced every bad thing that a child could've experienced, and I could not take it anymore. I started to imagine living with my father. I thought there was no way things could be worse. I didn't know anyone on my father's side of the family, and to me, that was a safer way to live. I would not have to go through any more abuse.

I still kept my grades up in school despite the distractions in my life. One day in the fifth grade the teacher asked, "Class, what is the opposite of include?" Everyone that answered gave the wrong answer, and that angered her because she had already given us the answer weeks ago. She reached for her leather belt and started walking around asking each one of us individually. Everyone that gave the wrong answer got hit with the belt. She would ask whether or not the person wanted to get hit in their hand or over the back. There were three rows in the classroom, and I was sitting in the back of the middle row. She went through the first row then the middle row, and finally, she got to me and asked, "what is the answer?" I replied, "exclude." She went on to say to the class, "class why can't you all be like Joseph?" I felt proud of myself for hearing her say that, but I thought to myself that I did not believe anyone in the class wanted my life. That day the kids in the row over got spared because of my answer, they all thanked me. I was always like an outsider, but this day everyone in my class was my friend. Feeling like an insider only lasted for a day. The next day things were back to normal. I was at the back of the class; everyone was pretending I was not there.

At the age of ten, I started to realize how poor we were. There were times we could barely afford food. My mother struggled to try to take care of my siblings alone and me. She decided to try and be with my younger sister's father, but they fought a lot. The fights would get so bad that the entire neighborhood would come out to watch as he beat on my mother. One day I remember watching him punch my mother in her face so hard that her teeth on her top and bottom rows fell out. Not only did my mother have several scars on her face from my father cutting her, but she was also now missing teeth. I wanted to protect my mother, but I was too little. I stood there unable to help when she needed me. I was not sad anymore; I was angry. I made a list of people I was going to kill when I got older, and my uncle was the first on the list for abusing me. My father was second for cutting my mother's face up as he did, and my sister's father was third for punching my mother's teeth out.

One Saturday evening, I was sitting in the front yard and heard my mother yell for me. I answered, and she said that she was making sure I was still in the yard. I began to act out around this time. I started having trouble coping with the things I saw and been through in my life. I left the yard without my mother knowing and I ran until I reached a tree. There was a fence made out of barbed wire running from one tree to another. I did not see it, and it caught me in my eyes. I was running fast, and so it pinned me back to the ground.

I got up and realized that I was unable to see from my left eye and I could feel and smell the blood running down my face. I took my shirt and covered my eyes immediately. I started to cry out for help. I thought I was blind because I could not see anything. A group of people were standing by the road and saw me coming toward them crying with my face covered in blood. They asked what was wrong. I took the shirt from my face, and one of the bystanders shouted, "Jesus Christ!" That put so much fear in me. I knew it had to be bad. I had no idea of how severe the injury was, but that was confirmation that it was terrible. A man riding a motorcycle was passing by and saw the crowd and decided to stop to see what happened. They told him that I got cut in my face and they thought I was blind. I started to think about my mother and how mad she would be. She told me not to leave the yard, and there I was with a group of strangers who believed that I was blind. He told me to get on his bike because he was going to take me to the hospital.

Once I arrived at the hospital, the nurse and doctor were curious about the injury. The doctor told me he did not know if I would be able to see out of my left eye again. I started to cry because everything that could ever go bad was going bad. The doctor stitched my face. I could feel the needle on my eyes. They could not numb my cuts because of its location on my face and was yelling from the pain. Until they finished stitching me, I had to endure the pain. When it was finally over, they covered my eye with bandages.

After the doctor finished stitching my eye, I went outside, and the guy that brought me to the hospital was there waiting for me. That was great because it was a long walk home from the hospital. On the way home all I could think about was my mother's reaction to seeing my face. I know she was looking for me and I was sure someone from the crowd already told her about what happened. Once I

arrived home, the first thing she said to me was, "didn't I

tell you not to leave the yard?" I stood there speechless

looking at her through my one eye. I was in excruciating

pain. Despite my current state, I expected a beating. I was

going to get one, but the guy that took me to the hospital

begged my mother not to beat me. He told her that there

was no way I could take any more pain. It worked because

she sent me straight to bed. I had to stay out of school for a

while; it took a lot of getting used to being only able to see

from one eye. It was constant pain and discomfort.

Weeks passed, and it was time to remove the

bandage. My mother took me to the hospital to have the

bandage removed. Once the doctor took off my dressing,

my eye would not open. The doctor asked me to open it. I

tried as hard as I could to open my eye, but it wouldn't

open. He wiped my eye off with an unknown solution and

shined a flashlight in my eye and asked if I saw anything. I told him yes because I could see a little, I was happy, but my eye was still sore. After he took the stitches out, I was able to go back to school. The first day I returned to school the kids saw the injury on my face and made fun of me. One name that stuck with me was V face. The injury shaped like a V because of the design of the barbed wire.

The other kids making fun of me of because of my scars added to the reasons I did not want to go to school. I started skipping school because I did not want to be there. I did not want the life I was living anymore. I was dirt poor, dark-skinned, and now a large scar on my face. I was the joke of the class. Since my house was behind the school, and the neighbors knew my mother. They would tell her if they saw me skipping school. I had to be extremely careful. It cost us to attend school in Jamaica, so if I got caught, I knew it would be one of the worst beatings. I would wait until the school bell rings for us to assemble. Then I would sneak off into the nearby bushes. I stayed there until lunch period and would go home for lunch my mother prepared.

After lunch, I would leave back out and go back to the bushes for the remaining of the school day. I would write in my books and makeup math problems and solve them as if it was school work given to me by my teacher. I would do English, Reading, and comprehension. I was making up stories and sentences and giving myself homework. After school was out, I would get out the bushes and walk home with my brother and sister. We all would go back and do homework as if we all went to school. I did that for a very long time. I would go to school three to four days out of the week to ensure my teacher saw me. I was doing that, so it would not alarm my teacher to get in contact with my mother. I also made sure I would pay attention to what subject the teacher was working on so that it would be easier to fabricate work when I did not go to school.

I finished primary school without any friends. One day after school I was walking home by myself as I did almost every day and I felt someone kick me so hard in my back that I fell forward on my face. I immediately attempted to get up, but on my way back up I felt another kick from the side. By the time I realized what was going on I was surrounded by four boys and they were all taking turns kicking me. I did not know these boys. I had only seen them around the schoolyard, but I had never spoken to or heard about them. Someone was attacking me; I had no clue what was going on. My house was close to the school, and I was trying to find an opening to run home.

Every time I tried to run they would kick me back to the ground. I remember the last kick I got that made me fall to one of the boy's feet. I looked up, and he was looking at his friends laughing. He wasn't paying attention to me, so I decided that was my chance to get away. It was the perfect opportunity, and I took it. I got up and ran as fast as I could. The boys chased me, but I kept running with everything inside me until I reached my gate. When I arrived at my gate, I looked back and saw they stopped chasing me. I cried until my eyes hurt. I did not feel safe anywhere, not at home or school. I felt as if I had no one to talk to about how sad, upset, and hurt I was. Life was a big disappointment.

The fifth-grade exams came around. These tests are ones that allow you to skip sixth grade and go straight to high school. In Jamaica, at that time you could only go to high school if you passed the exam if you failed they sent you to a secondary school. As kids, we called it the high school for rejects. I skipped school a lot and was worried that I would not pass the exams. High school was a big deal for my mother because no one in our entire family ever went to high school. I went into the exam room with no confidence. I was taking the test because my mother advised it. Luckily for me, as I begin taking the exam, I realized it was easy. I knew almost all the answers. After it was over, I went home, and my mother asked me how it went. I told her with slight confidence that I thought I did okay. Months went by, and the results came out. Everyone was excited and curious to see who passed the exam.

The results were in the day's newspaper, and everyone went and bought one. No matter how poor we were, we found money that day to buy a paper to see our names in the newspaper. My neighbor's daughter was in the sixth grade, and she took the exam. They already had a copy of the paper with the names. Her daughter made it, and they looked for my name and saw it. They started shouting at my mother, she yelled. "BLANCH YOUR BOY MADE IT!" My mother heard her screaming and rushed over to see. I heard them talking but as big as this was I was not excited, I did not care. I was the only boy that made it from the class of thirty-two students. One other girl made it, so it was just the two of us. I was the first person from my family going to high school, and my mother was so excited she walked around the entire community telling anyone that would listen. The school fee to go to high school in Jamaica is expensive for a lot of people, especially my mother. My mother went to have a conversation with my father about helping her with the expenses. My father was excited about the news that I was going to high school and promised he would help my mother.

MY SISTER'S RAPE

The summer before high school was one of my worst; it made me realize how weak I was. One Sunday my older sister and I went to the beach, it was about a ten to fifteen-minute walk from our home. There was a large crowd of people on the beach that day. I hated being around people, so I suggested that we walk and look for a less crowded spot. We walked until we were at the end of the beach where the river meets the ocean. There were a lot of bushes and fewer people, and it felt like the perfect spot for us to swim. We saw our uncle coming through the scrubs; this is the uncle that molested me. He called my sister in the bushes, and I watched her walk towards him. I wanted to tell her not to go, but I stood there and watched as she walked towards the bushes to him. I knew his exact plans for her. I saw him push her to the ground and get on top of her. He pulled my sister's clothes off and started to force himself on her. I stood and watched her cry and fight him off. I wanted to help, but I was so scared I didn't know what to do, I felt so helpless.

Luckily, some people walked by and saw what my uncle was doing and stopped to help her. My sister pulled her clothes up and ran by me as if she had forgotten that we came to the beach together. My sister and I have different fathers, and her father's family lived close to the beach. She ran in the direction of where they lived. Once my uncle realized my sister was older and smarter than me, he ran to avoid conflict. I walked home from the beach by myself. I was scared. I did not know what to think and how to process what I witnessed. When I got to my neighborhoods house, I saw a huge crowd gathered on the street. The group was a combination of my sister's father relatives and my neighbors. They came to do their village justice. Village justice is when the community takes the law in their own hands and be the judge and jury, and more often than not you get severely beaten or killed.

They wanted my uncle to explain to them what happened. They were armed with machetes, ready to take his life for what my sister told them he did to her. As I got closer to the crowd, I could hear the anger in their voices towards my uncle because he was unable to give a viable explanation. Once I reached the crowd my uncle saw me and called me over to him. "JOSEPH, COME HERE!!!" he said in a scared and frightened voice. He was crying out for help and needed me to save his life. He said, "JOSEPH, DID YOU SEE ME RAPE YOUR SISTER?" he knew I saw what happened, so I was confused about what answer he expected from me. I was silent for a minute while my heart filled with terror. My sister with tears running down her face needed someone to speak for her the same way I did when my uncle raped me.

My uncle realized that I was not saying anything, so he decided to demonstrate to my sister's family what he did. He laid me on the ground and put his knees in my chest. I was only ten years old, and this hurt and I was terrified. He then said to everyone. "This was what I did. I was playing with her. I never touched her like she's saying I did." He looked at me and yelled, "AM I LYING JOSEPH?" He was scaring me into lying for him. I looked at my sister's tear-filled eyes. I was brokenhearted because I love my sister, but my uncle scared me. He and my grandmother were the only two people that scared me to death.

I could feel the hurt and humiliation, the dirty feeling you get from being violated. I could feel the pain from being forcefully ripped open; from the betrayal by someone she trusted. I could see all that in my sister's eyes, because that was me a few years ago, except I had no one that stood up for me. It's the worst feeling ever having your innocence taken away from you by someone who was supposed to protect you. He asked me again in a louder and more stern and threatening tone; I started thinking about the time I spoke the truth and got beaten and called a liar. I said

in a soft voice, scared for my life, "yes." My uncle then

said, THERE YOU GO, TOLD YOU I WASN'T LYING!"

One of my sister's uncle told my uncle to stay away from

my sister. They all walked away and took my sister with

them. From that day forward my sister lived with her father

and the relationship we had as siblings were never the

same. We never talked about that day ever again. The hurt

and guilt from secrets I had inside haunted me for years. I

had nightmares of my uncle coming to get me in my sleep;

I lied to protect the man that raped my sister and me.

     The summer was coming to an end; it was almost

time for my first day of high school. I was still shaken up

from all that happened these past few months. I tried my

best to suppress all the bad memories and tried to look

forward to high school. The promises my father made to

my mother about helping her with the expenses for me to

go to high school was empty. When it was time for him to

help pay for the clothes, books, shoes, and backpack. He told her he didn't have any money. He had three months to prepare and was still unable to offer any assistance whatsoever. While there was excitement for my accomplishment, no one put forth the effort to ensure I had all I needed. No one made sure that I got help with my homework. It felt as if I was taking care of myself. I saw how proud my mother was. I don't think my mother expected anything great from us, but I decided to try. I didn't know what to expect. I didn't know how I would fit in knowing how scared I was of being around people.

I could never look anyone in their eyes. I felt they could see right through me and see all the secrets and pain I tried to keep inside. I was living in a very homophobic place, and any inkling of that would result in death or severe injuries. At that time I had already heard stories and witnessed people getting beaten by an entire community, or being chased out and forced to live on the streets or in bushes for any form of homosexual behavior. I did not agree with what happened to me. I could not protect myself, and I had no one to protect me. I was living in constant terror. I couldn't walk without looking behind me thinking my uncle or someone was coming to get me. I never felt safe.

HIGH SCHOOL

It was the first day in September and the first day of high school. My mother was able to purchase all the items I needed despite not having help from my father. I saw my mother crying while I was getting dressed for school; she was so proud that her son was going to high school. My first day of school went ok. My teachers introduced themselves, and they all seemed nice. I was open to trying because of the effort my mother was putting in to ensure I had all I needed. It became overwhelming for her, but she tried her best. She managed to come up with the money for bus fare and lunch every day. I would sometimes overhear her borrowing money from the neighbors or her friends just for me to go to school. At times I was embarrassed that she would have to ask for money. It felt like going to high school was a curse.

I remember one day she came home crying and could hardly get her words out. I was concerned about what happened; she told me that she asked my grandmother to loan her lunch money for me to go to school. She did not want me to miss any days. My mother said she witnessed my uncle giving my grandmother money the day prior, but just as my grandmother was reaching to loan my mother the money my uncle said, "MAMA IF YOU GIVE BLANCH ANY OF THAT MONEY I WILL NEVER GIVE YOU ANOTHER DOLLAR!" She told me that my grandmother said to her that she didn't have it to give. She burst into tears and a stranger passing by asked her what was wrong and she said to them that she needed lunch money for me to go to school and the stranger loaned her the money. When I heard that story and saw how it ripped my mother apart I was so hurt. I was determined to make my mother's life better. I have witnessed her go through so much.

My school was a thirty-minute bus ride from my home; it was hard for me being from a small town going into a big city. I was difficult getting used to the traffic and people walking around. It rained a lot, almost every day, and I would get wet. The buses would not let me get on unless I was dry. I would have to wait until the water dried up off my clothing to get on the bus, and sometimes that took a long time. When I got home on those days, it would be late, and my mother would be upset. I told her that the buses would not let me get on because I was wet, and it rained almost every day. She decided to buy me a raincoat to take to school. It became a life saver. I was now able to get home early before it got dark, and that made my mother happy.

One day on my way home from school I fell asleep on the bus. When the bus reached my destination, I got off the bus leaving behind the raincoat. When I got home, my mother realized that I was without the coat and immediately got upset. She asked me where it was. I knew I had it with me going on the bus, so I figured that's where it was. I told her I mistakenly left it on the bus. She said to me that if I came home without it the next day, I would get a beating. The following I decided to wait on the bus. The buses in Jamaica don't run on a schedule, so I had to wait a long time. The time for me to make it to school on time was going by fast. I was terrified that I would get a beating if I did not return home with the raincoat, so I waited.

Finally, I saw the bus coming. It stopped, and I got on it. I immediately went to the conductor and asked him if he had seen a raincoat left on the bus, he replied. "Yes." He said I should go to the driver of the bus because he had it. I went to the driver and asked him about the raincoat. He then pulled the bag with the coat from under his seat. I realized that the bag containing the coat had some holes in it. I figured that someone was looking inside the bag to see what was in it, so I paid no attention to the holes. I was late for school and missed the first class. I made it in time for gym class. I put my backpack in my classroom and put my gym clothes in the bag with the raincoat. I went outside to join the other kids.

I proceeded to change into my gym clothes, but while pulling my clothes out of the bag, something fell out on the ground. Other kids were standing around and saw that something fell from the bag. I looked and immediately realized that it was marijuana, so did the other kids. This one boy in-particular said he wanted it. I knew my mother smoked, so I told him no. I told him that I was taking it to my mother. He said that if I didn't give it to him that he was going to speak to the principal. I told him to go ahead. At the age of eleven, I had never smoked or even tried it. I figured I could say to the principal what happened, and she would believe me. The boy went to the principal. When he returned, he was with two older school boys.

When they arrived, they had a look as if I was in trouble. I knew I didn't do anything wrong, so I was not worried. I figured I'd tell the principal the truth, and she would take the marijuana, and that would be the end of it, but I was so wrong. She asked to see the marijuana. I showed it to her. She asked me where I got it from and why did I bring it to school. I told her it was not mine. It fell out of the bag that held my raincoat that I left on the bus. She said she did not believe me and I should tell her the truth. I repeated what I said to her because it was the truth. She told me, "Joseph I am going to have you go home and get your parents."

I knew I was telling the truth. I did not think that there would be any repercussions. When I got home, I told my mother what happened. We were both optimistic because we knew I did not smoke. I used to beg my mother to quit smoking; I was not a fan of smoking. The following day my mother and I went to school together to meet with the principal. She called us into the office, and asked my mother, "do you know what your son does when he's not with you?" She showed my mother the marijuana and told her that I was smoking. With tears in her eyes, my mother said, "no, Joseph does not smoke and a matter of a fact he begs me every day to quit." I repeated what I told her that it was in the bag, and I had no clue how it got there. The only reason I didn't give it to the other kid was that I was going to give it to my mother because she used it. She said she had no choice but to expel me from school. The look on my mother's face was of disappointment, hurt, and heartbreak. My mother believed me, but no one else did. Her first child that made it to high school was about to unfairly lose the opportunity of an education.

The feeling of injustice was unbearable and watching my mother cry to the principal begging her not to expel me, broke my heart. We both wept to the principal. I kept repeating that I was not lying. Once again I was telling the truth to someone that was supposed to protect and teach me, and they were calling me a liar. They were about to take away my only opportunity to get an education. I questioned the reason for telling the truth since there was never anything beneficial from being honest. I got beat and punished every time. The principal said shew would give me a two week suspension instead. Even though suspension was better than getting expelled it still felt wrong getting punished for something I didn't do. I could not believe what was happening. It felt like a nightmare, and that feeling of injustice made me bitter and angry. They were teaching me to lie at that moment. Leaving the schoolyard, I decided that I was giving up. I felt there was no hope for me. I was tired of getting abused mentally, physically, and sexually. I was tired of getting beaten, lied to, and lied on. I was tired of not being trusted when all I needed was just one person to be there for me. I did not care who it was I just needed someone there, but there was no one. I always felt alone, and this situation made it worse.

After my mother and I got home, I changed my clothes and went to my favorite place, the hills, a place where I could watch the wind blow the trees. It was just

God and nature, and I remembered praying that day asking

God why I was going through all of this? Why is everyone

hurting me? Why is everyone I trust betraying me? In the

hills it was so peaceful with no one around; I didn't want to

go back home. I thought about all the abuse I was going

through and the secrets I was keeping. During the two

week's suspension from school, I did not believe that I was

going back to school and I did not care.

When it was time for me to back to school, I woke

up, got ready, and left. I did not know where I was going,

but I knew I was not going back to school. I walked to

town, and on my way, I started thinking of places I could

go. The distance between school and my house was a little

over thirty miles one way; I figured if I walked the thirty

miles back and forth, then it would take me all day as if I

went to school. As I was walking, I thought if someone saw

me, they would tell my mother, but then I thought that I

always got whippings, I did not care anymore. I walked ten miles, almost half the way to my school, then walked back home. I used the money my mother gave me for lunch and bus fare to buy food and drinks along the way. I did that for the entire first week back from suspension. I would leave home every day and walk several miles.

The following week, I felt the walk was too long. I needed something to do or somewhere to go that was much easier than walking so much, so I decided to go to the beach. While walking on the beach, I saw this older guy from the neighborhood. He said he was going fishing and told me that if I came along, I would get a lot of fish. I decided to go with him. I didn't know how to fish, but I thought it was easy. We spent all day fishing, and I didn't catch any fish, but the guy caught a lot. It was getting dark, and it was time for me to go back home. I asked the guy if I could get any of the fish since I went with him and I didn't catch any. He said yes, but he gave me the two smallest fishes he had. I thought to myself this was not fair.

I remembered that it was at that exact moment that I had decided that I was not taking any more crap from anyone. I was going to stand up for myself even if it cost me my life. The guy went home with the fish and I followed him and waited for him to go inside his house. He left the fish on a table outside, and I went in his yard and stole every single one and went home. My sister saw me coming and told me that my mother knew I didn't go to school. She has been preparing to give me a beating.

When I reached home, my mother grabbed my arm real tight. She started crying. She asked if I knew what she had to do to borrow money to send me to school to get an education so that I could turn out better in life than she did. I didn't answer, and she started beating me with an extension cord. Every time she hit me, I felt the wire rip through my skin. When she got done, she told me to go and take a shower and go to bed. We had no inside plumbing, so we used containers with water to bathe outside.

My mother came out and saw that I was not taking bathing. She asked if I wanted another beating, but I told her my skin had cuts all over I was unable to use soap because it burned when I touched my skin. She took the rag and soap from me and bathed me herself. It was painful; every area she touched had an open wound from the beating. When I woke up the next morning, I was in more pain than the night before. All the cuts were burning. I was still not going to school; I didn't care what was going to happen to me. I continued to leave as if I were going to school. I took the bus and went to the town my school was in and walked into every store that was there until I knew the school was out. When it was time for me to go back home, I got on the bus with everyone else from school and rode home. When I got home, my mother asked if I went to school and I told her that I did. She asked to see what I did in school that day. I had already fabricated my school work, and I showed it to her, but she didn't believe me.

Someone saw me in town and told her. She told my stepfather to go to my school to speak to my teacher and find out if I went to school that day. I prayed long and hard that night that he didn't find out that not only did I not go to school, but I didn't go the previous day either. I hadn't gone to school for over two weeks. The next day, I made sure I went straight to school. Around the second period; I saw my stepfather walk inside my class. I knew he was coming, but I was hoping he didn't show. My teacher called me to the front of the class; my stepfather was having a conversation with her. I heard him ask her to borrow the leather belt that she used to beat the kids in her class. He told me that my teacher informed him that I had not been to school in weeks and he wanted to know where I'd been going. He said he knows my mother sent me to school every day. I had no response.

He told me to open my hands, so I did. Then he started hitting me in the middle of my hands. He was beating me so hard that at one point I could not feel my fingers, so I pulled away from my hands and put them behind me. I could not hold them out anymore. He still wanted to hit me; I couldn't take the pain. Since I would not hold out my hands, he started beating me all over my back and wherever he could find a place to hit. Everyone in the classroom started laughing. I could hear the chuckles. I was in pain. My body hurt, and I was humiliated. After that day, there was no more doubt in my mind that I wanted to kill myself. I went through the entire day with everyone laughing at me. Everyone heard the news on what happened, and they all were pointing and laughing. Everyone was making fun of the fact that I just got beaten by my stepfather in front of my class.

On the bus ride home, the kids from my school told the kids from other schools, and they too made fun of me.

When I reached home, my mother was waiting for me. My stepfather had already arrived home and gave her the news of me skipping school. She had a fan belt that she got from out of an old car and used it to beat me. She was hitting me so hard; I couldn't take it anymore. I begged her please to take me to the juvenile detention center. I told her I would rather be in jail than to be with my family. I pleaded with her to take me to the police station because I did not want that life anymore. I did not want to be around anyone in my family. My mother decided to take me to the police station to tell them I was not going to school. She was going to tell them that she was unable to raise me because I was too much for her to handle. She wanted them to put me in a center for troubled kids. On our way to the station, we saw a guy from the neighborhood. He saw my mother dragging me through the street and stopped her to ask her where she is taking me. She told him that she was unable to control me and that I was misbehaving and not going to school.

Everyone was watching as I cried. I didn't know what to expect, but I figured anywhere was better than staying home with my family. I just wanted to be away from them. I was ruined by the people that were supposed to love me. At that point, I would rather be in prison than to be around them. The man told my mother that she should take me back home and beat me and she did. It was one of the worst beatings I had ever gotten from my mother; it was so painful. When it was finally over, I couldn't move from where I lay. I stayed there crying for almost an hour.

The next day I got dressed for school and left out of the house knowing that I was never going back to school. I remembered that I had a family member that lived in another part of the country and I decided that I would go there. I didn't know exactly where they lived, but I figured I would find out. I got on the bus and rode for almost two hours. I asked the conductor to notify me when I reached the town that my family lived. I got off the bus and walked

No Love

to the first store I saw. I went in and asked if they knew my family, and fortunately, they did. They told me that it was far away, about two miles walking. I was used to walking, so two miles was easy for me. They gave me the directions, and I found my family's house.

They were happy to see me, but they wanted to know what I was doing there on a school day. I lied and told them I that was suspended from school, and my mother said I could be there. I told them that the reason I was wearing my school clothes was that it cost less to travel as a student on the bus. After staying with my family for three days, I overheard one of them on the phone and the way the conversation was going it sounds as if they were talking to my mother. She was telling them that sent me to school and hadn't seen me in two days and called everyone she knew, and they told her I was there. She said she would take the next bus to come and get me. When she arrived, I saw the look on her face; I knew that look, I was in a lot of trouble when I get home. She told me that she thought I was dead and that she had been distraught. Although seeing my mother cry broke my heart, I was going through so much hurt myself. I just wanted to be away from everyone; I never felt safe nor protected. When we got home, I got a beating from my mother and as much pain as I felt by getting the beating the pain inside was worse. The next day, I overheard my stepfather bragging about beating me. I was mad.

I was still skipping school, and would only go when I had no place else to go, and it started to get harder. I was so far behind. The times I would go to class I had no idea what my teacher was teaching. My first year of high school ended and the report card came out and was not as bad as I thought it would be. I still managed to get a B after missing so many classes. Summer came along, and I stayed to myself.

One day during the summer my stepfather told me to get him water from the pipe that was about half a mile from the house, after hearing him bragging about beating me I decided not to. I told him no, he and chased me. I ran as fast as I could, but I could not outrun him. He caught me and started beating me with a piece of board. He was hitting me all over I started yelling for my mother. I asked her if she was going to let my stepfather beat me. She stayed inside and didn't say anything, so he beat me until he was satisfied, then he let me go. I ran as fast as and as far away as I could. I was crying and getting so mad; my hurt and pain turned into anger. At that time everything changed. I decided I wasn't going to take it anymore. I saw this broken wheelbarrow on the side of the street. I picked it up and filled it with rocks. I put in as many as I could.

The wheelbarrow was packed with rocks; with tears running down my face, I headed straight for home; I'd had enough of everyone taking advantage of me. When I reached the house, I emptied the wheelborrow and had the rocks stacked on the ground. I started throwing rocks at the house and cursing telling my stepfather to come outside so I could kill him. He rushed out to beat me, but he wasn't prepared for my retaliation. I had a lot of rocks, so as soon as he stepped outside, I started to throw them at him repeatedly. He ran back inside the house. My mother was inside the house and yelled at me to stop and behave myself. I told her I would not stop because she stood there and watched everyone take advantage of me and did nothing. I was too angry at that point. I wanted to hurt someone, and I did not care who it was.

I stood at the gate with rocks in my hands for a while. I told my stepfather to come outside so I could kill him. He stayed inside until it was dark. I knew the severity of what I just did. I knew there would be hell to pay, but I did not care anymore. I felt it was a fight I had to have. I felt as if I was fighting for my life. I had to figure out

where I was going to sleep because going back inside the
house after what I just did was not an option. I went up into
the hills where I always go. Under some bushes, I made a
bed out of fallen coconut tree branches. It started to get
really dark. I laid down on my back looking up at the stars
praying; asking God for help. "Why am I here oh God,
what have I done to deserve this life? I have no peace; no
one loves me." I kept repeating that prayer. I prayed that
one day my life would change. I couldn't sleep; I was up all
night. Normally I would be scared of being in the bushes
late at night, but I was feeling angry. That made me brave
when the day started to break my body was shutting down,
and eyes would not stay open. I slept for a while; when I
woke up I felt hungry, so I climbed one of the coconut trees
and picked some coconuts. I picked enough to last me
because I knew that that was going to be my homeless for
some time. I stayed in the bushes for a few days. I figured
it was time to go to town to see what was going on.

When I got to the house, I saw my mother and stepfather arguing about me. I went inside the house and saw his stuff packed. They were breaking up. It was never my intentions to ever chase anyone away from my mother. I could not take the abuse anymore; everyone was taking a turn on abusing me. I took a bath outside and went straight to sleep. My mother didn't say anything to me, and I didn't say anything. Months went by; and it was time to go back to school. With my stepfather gone and my father not helping my mother didn't have any money to get any new school uniforms or shoes. I grew a lot over the summer, and she was a dressmaker, so she improvised and added pieces of materials to the shirts and pants I had for school. She put them together and made two complete sets. The additions to my clothes were noticeable. There was no way of hiding it. I tried to blend in as much as possible at school, but it was impossible for others to ignore.

One day I was in class the boy sitting behind me saw that my shirt was old and it had additions to it. He called the entire class to look at my shirt and pants; they all came laughing and pointing. Their nickname for me from that day was "extension." Everywhere I went to school they would laugh and point at me calling me "Extension". I cried; it was embarrassing. I was poor, and there was nothing I could do about it. No one wanted to be my friend. I went home that day crying telling my mother that I was not going back to school. I told her everyone was making fun of me. She said to me that I should bear out the next two weeks and she would try and see if she could get me a shirt.

Two weeks went by; they were the longest weeks I had ever had at school. The kids teased, pointed at, and talked about me every day. My mother borrowed money from one of her friends to purchase my new uniforms. She asked if I would like to transfer schools, and I told her yes.

I wanted to be away from that school. My mother got a transfer for me; I was open-minded. I figured it was a fresh start. I didn't expect life to be great, but I wanted some peace. I prayed it was a school with regular kids who would not bully me. My first day was uneventful. I didn't make any friends, but I didn't feel out of place. I saw a few kids to themselves just like I usually was, and no one was bothering them. My new school was peaceful, and I decided to give it a try, but a few months later my mother met a guy from another town. He promised to take care of her, but she would have to move to live with him. At the time my mother was in a court proceeding trying to get child support from my father.

LIVING WITH MY FATHER

When I was thirteen, my mother made a deal with my father regarding me; she told him that if he took me in she would drop the child support case. It seemed like a great idea to my father. He wouldn't have to pay any money. My mother took my brother and sisters and left me behind. Once again I felt abandoned, neglected, and unloved. I was heartbroken; it felt as if my heart was in several pieces. I felt my mother thought I would be trouble for her new relationship because of my behavior. My mother was leaving me with the man who did some horrible things to her. Though he was my father, he was not fit to raise a child. But I was a problem for my mother. I was sad and angry; no one saw how much I was hurting. I felt no one cared. I was crying out for help, but no one was listening, and it got worse every day. The living conditions in my father's place were deplorable. My father had not made any preparation for me. He had one job, and that was to raise me into a man, but he failed horribly.

My father carved souvenirs for tourists coming to Jamaica. He would make little guitars and drums from wood and bamboo with the colors of the Jamaican national flag painted on them. Some days he would make a lot of money, and that was all he bragged about every day. I would hear him bragging to anyone who would listen about how much money he was making. I wondered to myself every time I heard him talking: How could he allow his children to suffer for so long if he is making all that money? There were days when we had no food, no clothes, no lunch for school, and once I lived with him I saw the reason. The first night with my father he left at about ten pm. There was only one bed, and I had no idea what the living arrangements would be, so I slept in his bed. That night he slept at his girlfriend's house. I thought he would be sleeping with his lady at nights or buy me a bed considering the amount of money he claimed he was making. But the following night he gave me three sheets and some old clothing to use as a pillow. I had to lay two sheets on the floor, used the third one as a cover, and used the old clothing as my pillow. I thought that was temporary.

I was the only responsibility he had. My mother dropped the child support case after he agreed to take care of me. A few months after moving in with him I figured out why he was not able to help us and why he was unable to take care of me after I moved in with him. He was trying to impress his lady. When he met her, she was living with her mother, and to get her he had to provide a place for her to stay. That was where all of his money and attention was going. He was making a house for her while I was sleeping on the floor and walking around barefoot. One day turned into one week, then one month, then years. My father had me living with him, and every night I went to sleep on the floor with the three sheets and some old clothing for a pillow.

A year later at age fourteen, it was coming on to Christmas. I had never received a Christmas present; I saw other kids getting gifts. I used to wonder what it felt like opening up a gift. I knew I was poor, but I would have taken anything. It didn't matter what it was. I asked my father if he could buy me a pair of shoes for Christmas. He said I would have to work with him for two weeks. For the next two weeks, I worked with my father right through the day and half the night. I didn't know what shoes I wanted, but it would be my first pair and my first Christmas present. The two weeks went by, and it was the day before Christmas Eve. It was time for my father to sell the products we worked on for the previous two weeks.

My father took me to Kingston with him; he wanted to show me how he sells his carvings and how much money he would make. He got a check for twenty-five thousand

Jamaican dollars, that was a lot of money in Jamaica for someone as poor as we were. He bragged to me telling me that I could make all that money one day. For once in my life I was so excited, I could not remember being that excited for anything. My father and I walked to a nearby clothing and shoe store. I remembered walking in the store, and the first thing I saw was a pair of Reebok Classics. They were white with blue on the bottom and were on sale, for two thousand Jamaican dollars. I asked my father if he could use the money he was supposed to pay me to purchase the shoes. He said yes, but he would have to wait until the bank opened the next day to cash the check to buy the shoes. On our way home I was so excited I started to think maybe my father was not that bad after all. My father was about to give me my first ever Christmas present.

I couldn't sleep that night all I could think about was wearing those Reeboks. I kept thinking that no one would make fun of me anymore for walking barefoot. The following morning my father got up early and left. I had to carry water from a spring that was pretty far away, but that morning I got up and made as many trips to the spring to fill every container available. I did the dishes and waited for my father to get home. It was getting dark, I was too excited to wait at home, so I walked down the street to see if I could meet my father on his way home. There were two paths to walk to the house from the town. I walked the first pathway until I almost reached town, then I stopped and turned back. I started to think maybe he got held up in traffic or maybe he walked the other route to the house. I decided to walk back home.

When I reached home I saw some bags sitting on the floor I knew he came home. I immediately rushed towards the bags and started searching for the shoes. I didn't see the shoes, but there was food in the bag. I took out some of the food and started eating because I had not eaten all day. I yelled out for my father, but there was no answer. I could not find the shoes, but we had a deal so in my mind I thought that maybe my father hid the shoes. I thought he was going to surprise me for Christmas just like in the movies. I called out his name again and still no answer. He was not home, but I knew that whenever he got the money he usually went over to his girlfriend's house. I figured I would wait until he got home.

The next day I was sleeping by the door when I heard it open. I got up looking at him with excitement in my eyes waiting for my surprise. He walked by me laying on the floor as if we did not have an agreement. It was as if he didn't remember the promise he made to me, so I asked him, "Daddy where are the shoes?" He replied, "I am sorry; I couldn't get to buy them," I said to him, "let's go get them now." He said he did not have any money, that he promised his girlfriend money to buy furniture for her new place for Christmas. Those words broke my heart into a thousand pieces. I started crying; I cried out so loud. It was as if someone was beating me. Everyone in my life chose everything and everyone else over me. My happiness meant nothing to no one. I never felt loved or believed that I was important to anyone. I asked him if he was ever going to pay me for the work I'd done. He said, "NO!" He said that he was already feeding me, so it evens itself out.

I felt robbed and cheated by my father. I worked for him and he did not pay me. On Christmas, I watched all the kids from the neighborhood as they played with their toys and showed what clothes and shoes they got. My father's girlfriend's kids also managed to get Christmas gifts, but I did not get anything. I cried all night on Christmas. I wanted to leave my father's house, but I had no place to go. I felt as if I was raising myself. My father would work during the week then on the weekends, would sell his craft then come home put his stuff down and go off to his girlfriend's house. He would come back a few days later with no money. She took all his money, sometimes all he would have was a few dollars. Enough to send me to school three or four days out the five days I should be in school. I used to wonder if his girlfriend was the reason I was able to go to school. I felt she was the one letting him keep some of the money for me to go to school. I felt like my life was going to waste. I had no clue what I was going to do with my life, and I had no direction. My father didn't care what happened to me; he just had me there to get out of paying child support. He could not wait until I was eighteen, so he wouldn't have me as a responsibility.

As a way to deal with my life, I started playing soccer by myself. I would make a ball by combining drink boxes that I found on the ground. I would kick it around on the street; if I were going to the store, I would kick the makeshift ball to and from the store. I would imagine myself playing for my favorite soccer team making the winning play and celebrating. I lived in my imagination a lot because my life and everyone in it was hurtful. I started going to the park to watch the older guys play. I tried to see their tricks and how they played, then I would go home and get my ball and practice. I did that for a long time, but one day I went to the park to watch the older guys play, and they were short a player. They saw me sitting there watching them, and one of the guys asked me if I wanted to play. At first, I was scared, but I said yes. That day was my first time playing soccer with others. I was watching them, so I tried to do the things I saw them doing. It was fun, but I was not as good as I imagined. I decided to start going more often, so I could learn more. I started learning to play better; soccer quickly became an outlet for the daily pain and anger I was holding inside.

MY FIRST GIRLFRIEND

The summer I turned fifteen I met a young girl. I liked her, but I knew nothing about affection or love. I'd never seen or experienced it. I had an idea, or I thought I did, by the things I'd seen on TV. I used to dream about finding the girl of my dreams and living happily ever after. Before I met her, I did not want my life anymore. I was having a constant battle in my mind with myself. I was getting so bitter as I grew older remembering everything that happened. I made a promise to myself that if and when I found a girl I would marry her, and I would never hurt or leave her. We would have kids, and I would love them and protect them with all my life. I wanted to give my wife and kids the life I never had.

The girl was a year younger than I was, but she was more experienced. I'd never had sex before, but she was very promiscuous. She would sleep around every chance she got, and somehow I would find out from people talking.

When I confronted her, she would cry, and I would forgive her. She would sleep around so often I started to look forward to her cheating. I knew nothing about love, but I felt she needed me, and I needed her. I had nothing in my life worth holding to; no good childhood memories, no best friends, no family that cared and a father who had no love or guidance to give.

My life was empty, and even though she was hurting me by sleeping around, as long as she was coming back, I was ok. I thought she was the only one for me. I thought sex was the only way of showing love, so I thought she loved me. I would cry to her telling her how much I loved her. I figured if she saw how much I cared she would not hurt me anymore. I did not have any money, and I could not afford to give her what she needed, but I tried. She needed lunch sometimes, and she would send her cousins to me for food or money. I didn't want her cheating or asking someone else, so I would go looking for empty

glass bottles to exchange for cash to buy her lunch.

Sometimes I would save my food and not eat so that

I could give it to her when she needed it. I would steal

money from my father's pocket every month to buy her the

things she needed for her monthly cycle. I would

sometimes go to the store and tell the owner that my father

said to give me food and he would pay for it later, which

was never true. I just wanted to hold on to the only person I

thought loved me. I was doing anything and everything to

ensure she stayed. I did everything I could to make the

relationship last for as long as I could. The same cycle

continued nothing changed. She would sleep with someone

else, then she would be right back to me in a couple of

days, and I was stealing to maintain the relationship. When

I turned 16, my past started to bother me more than usual. I

started becoming more aware and thinking about the things

I experienced and saw them play out in my head. I first

started to process what my uncle did to me. I started questioning whether or not I showed him a sign that made him believe it was ok for him to hurt me. I wondered if I said or did something that made him think that what he did was ok and that I wanted him. If he saw a sign what was it? I wanted to know because if I did show him a sign I wanted to make sure it stopped. I wanted to make sure no one else looked at me and thought that way or tried to rape me again.

I had a constant battle in my mind just trying to figure out what to do, and I had no one to whom I could talk about my feelings. I came up with the idea which I thought at the time was brilliant. I figured that if I slept with as many girls as possible, no one would ever see any signs or assume that I wanted to be with a man. I figured that would work; no one would look at me and get the wrong idea. At sixteen years old I was still just the scared little seven-year-old boy inside crying out for help with no help in sight. I started on a journey; I was sleeping with any and every girl that would make themselves available. I just wanted the world to see that I was sleeping with a lot of women, and I did not like what my uncle did to me. I had a routine where I would go to a girls home when her parents were not there. At one point, I was having sex with four girls at the same time. I would go to the first one's home at about seven in the morning; her parents left for work early in the morning, and she attended school in the evenings. She had time in the morning to see me. After I left the first girls house, I would go to the second one's home at about ten in the morning; because she did not go to school. She was a bit older but still lived at home with her parents. I would go to the third ones home at noon. Her father worked a lot, so she was almost always home by herself. Then I would go to the last one's place at two in the afternoon. Her school let out at noon while her parents were still at work. I was doing that for a long time. Sex and soccer were what I used to block out my feelings about being sexually abused.

One day I was leaving one of the second girl's home, I knew the neighbors saw me leaving, so they started watching the home. They saw me coming and going almost every day. They told the girl's father about what they'd seen. One day when I was over the girl's house, I heard the keys in the door. I asked her if she was expecting anyone and she said no, and that I should hide. I jumped out the back door and hid behind the bushes in the back. I didn't know who it was, but I wasn't ready to leave, so I stayed around. I was waiting for whoever it was to leave, but that was a bad idea. It was her father; he pretended as if he was going to work then came home at the time the neighbors told him I would be there. I heard him coming through the back door asking his daughter where I was. She told him that there was no one there. I heard him coming closer to where I was so I got up and ran. He saw me and started yelling at me saying he was going to kill me if I ever came back to his house.

While I was running away I could hear him beating his daughter; on the street was looking at me. We all could hear the girl crying from the beating she was getting. A few hours later someone came to me and said I needed to find somewhere and hide. I asked them why. They told me that the girl's father was on his way to the police station because the girl said I was trying to rape her. I was speechless. I knew that was all lies, but knowing how things never go my way I figured this was it for me. I had nowhere to run, and I knew no one ever believed me and no one cared about my safety. I believed that the girl's father knew I didn't try to rape his daughter. He was just humiliated by the fact that his daughter was taking boys in his house. She wanted her father to stop beating her, so she told him I was trying to rape her.

The girl's mother saw me walking on the street and asked me what happened. I told her the truth; I told her that I'd been having sex with her daughter. I told her that she was my girlfriend of almost six months. I told her I was only there because she said I could come over, and we did that almost every day. The girl's father took her to the police station, and the police took her to the doctor. While the doctor was checking her out, she told him that the sex was consensual, and the doctor relayed that message to the police. They could not charge me for statutory rape since we were both sixteen. I did not expect to get out of that situation because no one ever believed my truth.

A couple of months later I met a new girl; everyone talked about her sleeping around. No one had ever talked to me about safe sex; after our first sexual encounter, I woke up the following day finding it hard to pee. It was very painful I couldn't stand. I saw stuff coming from my private area. I was scared and embarrassed. I did not know what to do, and I had no one to talk to about what was happening. There was this man that walked through the neighborhood every morning to go to the beach. People called him "doctor"a, so I waited for him the next day. I stopped him and started a conversation with him; I described to him what was happening to me. He told me to see him at the hospital, and to also bring the girl with whom I had sex. I saw the girl and told her what was happening and what the doctor said. She got upset and said she didn't have an STD. It was embarrassing for me, so I figured she was also embarrassed. The following morning I went to see the doctor by myself. The line was so long; I had to wait a while to see him. It surprised me to see so many people trying to see the STD doctor.

It was finally my time to see him. He asked me where the girl was, and I told him that she said she didn't have an STD and she didn't want to come. He proceeded to treat my symptoms. He took out this long needle, the longest I have ever seen and said, "this will be painful. Where do you want it, in your leg or on your butt cheek?" I told him on my butt cheek, and he stuck the needle in me so hard. It hurt so bad I could not move. He told me I could sit for a while and I should stay away from sex for seven days. He gave me a huge box of condoms and said, "use these." The hospital was a couple of miles from where I lived, and I did not have cab fare, so I had to walk. The pain from the injection was excruciating. What normally took me thirty minutes, took me an hour and a half to get home. The experience at the doctor changed my entire thought process. In a matter of months I could've gone to jail for something I was not guilty of, and I could've gotten an incurable disease.

MY FIRST BORN

When my mother moved away she left our home vacant. I was getting frustrated with my father's behavior and how he was treating me. I felt as if I could do better on my own. I decided to go live in my mother's vacant house. It was a poor man's home, but it was a roof over my head. There was no power or water, just a bed, some chairs, and a table. Living alone felt freeing, but it also brought the feeling of being alone alive. I was still seeing my first girlfriend; she would stay with me whenever she had nothing else to do. A couple of months went by, and she got pregnant. At sixteen I was about to be a father. No one taught me how to be a father, nor how to love and protect a child, but I knew I couldn't do what my father did. Finding jobs in Jamaica is hard, but I decided I would do anything to take care of my child. Her mother got upset with her and told her that I had to find somewhere for her to stay. I told her to stay with me.

I had an uncle who worked construction, I went to him and explained to him that I was expecting a baby and I needed a job and told him that I needed to save money for the baby; I needed baby clothing and other neccessities. He gave me a job, and I was able to buy food for us and save for the baby. The construction jobs don't last year round, so I saved as much as I possibly could. I would take her to her doctor visits every time she had to go. Being a responsible father felt great. I could not see why my father was not there for us; months went on, and I became more excited. I started dreaming about the father I would be. I wanted to make sure my child did not feel the way I did about my father. I wanted to be there in every way and make sure I did everything not to break the heart of my child. It was time for us to find out the sex of the baby. I was so happy I did not care what the sex was. I was willing to love and protect my child with everything in me. The things that had happened to me as a child still weighed heavily on my mind. I was wanted to make sure my child never had to go through what I did.

We went to the doctor for the ultrasound and found out it was a boy. I told my girlfriend not to do anything; I wanted to keep her safe so there would be no complications during the pregnancy. The job with uncle had ended, and I started going out every day trying to find another job. We had a little money saved, but I knew we needed more. I would cook for her in the morning to last her while I was gone. On some days I would get water from the neighborhood pipe and do our laundry by hand. I knew it would be hard, but I knew I would do my best to be a great father and a great husband because of the things I have seen and been through I knew what not to do. I picked out the name Akeem for him. It was from my favorite movie

"Coming to America." I would tell everyone that would listen that my son was going to be a prince.

In the sixth month of our pregnancy, one night my girlfriend was feeling pain. From the movies I'd seen I was not going to take any chances. She was feeling unbearable pain, and it was late. I ran out to the street to see if I could get a taxi, but I did not see one. I had left her by herself, so I didn't want to stand and wait for one to come. I quickly ran home and told her I didn't see any taxi. I told her that we should walk to the hospital which was about three miles from where we lived. I was hoping that while we were walking on the road, I would see a taxi that would stop and pick us up. We didn't see a taxi, so we slowly walked until we got to the hospital. I quickly ran inside and called a nurse letting her know that I thought my girlfriend was in labor. The nurses ran out to get her and brought her to a room. I was trying to follow them, but they stopped me and told me I had to wait outside. Hours past and I couldn't hear anything or see anyone coming. My little sister was born prematurely at seven months and was fine, so I wasn't worried.

Finally, a doctor came out and asked if I was the father of the baby. I said yes, he brought me to a room to show me, my son. He was only two and a half pounds. He was in an incubator and was unable to breathe on his own. My eyes filled with tears of joy. I was happy to see my son but sad that I could not hold him, and that he had to be in the incubator. The doctor told us that they had seen babies grow up to be healthy and strong from being in that situation, so I was very optimistic.

I had to leave the baby and my girlfriend in the hospital that day. I would go to the hospital every day with food and clothes for my girlfriend. I'd help her shower and get dressed, and then I'd see the baby. Every morning I would make sure to wash my girlfriend's clothes, cook then walk the three miles to the hospital. I would spend all day with them, that was the happiest time of my life. When it was time for my girlfriend to leave the hospital, we had to leave without Akeem. He was not fully developed, but I still was optimistic that I was going to have a family — something I'd always wanted, I had so much love inside me. I could not wait to give it to my child. My girlfriend and I started making a daily trip to the hospital. I was no longer filled with bitterness and hate. My past was not on my mind anymore; I had something to look forward to I had someone to love, my son and girlfriend. They were all I had, and I cherished every moment we spent together.

One day when we got to the hospital, we went to the newborn area like we always did, and we noticed the incubator was empty. I was happy; I figured Akeem was finally ready to go home with us. I rushed to the nurse's station with a big grin on my face and asked one of the nurses where he was. She told us that his heart stopped beating, and they had to rush him to do immediate surgery.

It felt like a huge brick wall just fell on my entire body and crushed my heart. I cried out so loud everyone started looking at me, but I did not care. I immediately prayed, "God, please let Akeem be ok," I said it three times then I looked over at my girlfriend, and she was also crying. They told us to wait in the waiting room until the doctor came to see us.

We waited impatiently then finally we saw the doctor coming. We both anxiously sat praying for some good news. When the doctor came to us he said, "there is no easy way to say this…" I immediately knew that I was notgoing to like what he had to say next. He told us that our baby died before he had the chance to operate on him. My girlfriend and I cried together. I hugged her and told her I was sorry. I needed a hug also and for someone to tell me it would be ok, but I know my girlfriend needed me more. The doctor asked us what we wanted to do with the body. I knew it was a conversation that they needed have with us, but we weren't ready\. I'd been through so much, and this was something I was looking forward to.

I wanted to be a father. I had so much love to give, but at that time all I had inside me was pain. We decided to go home; my girlfriend could not stop crying. I wanted to be strong for her, so I was holding back my tears. My heart was so heavy, my eyes were hurting, and my throat was blocked. I was choking trying to hold back from crying. We told the doctor that we would be back the next day, but he told us that they could cremate the body if we did not want to go through the expenses of a funeral. My girlfriend did not want to go through the pain of a funeral, so she agreed to the cremation . I didn't want to agree because I was already attached to Akeem. I had everything figured out. I was going to teach him how to be a man, and how to play soccer. He was never going to need anything I was trying to be a good father to him. I saw the pain my girlfriend was going through, so I finally agreed. When we got home, our relationship was never the same. We both were hurt watching each other cry. We would lay in bed all day feeling sorry for ourselves. The grief of losing a child, of seeing him born, and then suddenly gone was unbearable.

A couple of weeks later the grief started to turn into anger. My girlfriend started saying that she thought the doctors couldn't bother with treating our baby, so they stopped his heart on purpose. I didn't want to believe that, so I told her to stop saying such things. We had a huge fight going back and forth about it. She decided she wanted to go home back to her mother; I didn't want her to go, but I was grieving and I told her I didn't care. She started packing all her stuff saying she didn't want to be with me anymore. I told her I didn't care, but deep down inside I needed her to stay. I couldn't get it out; I just stood there while she packed her things. She asked me for help with her stuff to take to her mother's, I did.

On the way walking through the town, we didn't say a word to each other. The loss of the baby had torn us apart. We got to her mother's place, and her family was all sitting outside. Her mother saw the look on her face and asked her what was wrong. My girlfriend replied that the baby had died. Her mother said, "that is God telling you that you and Joseph should not be together." Those words were some of the most hurtful words I' ever heard. I was speechless; I just stood by the gate holding my girlfriend's stuff while she put away what she had in her hand. She came back to get the rest of her stuff that I was holding. I went home, and the feeling of losing everything was looming over me. I felt sad; I stayed in bed for three days. There was no food in the house, but I had no desire to eat anything.

After spending so many days by myself; I started to think about my ex-girlfriend I knew how hard it was for her. I decided to see her and see how she was doing. When

I got there, she was inside her house, so I called her. I could

hear the excitement in her voice when she answered. She

rushed out and hugged me so tight; I guess she missed me

too. She asked me what was I doing there, and I told her

that I came to see how she was doing. She said that she

wanted to come home with me. I needed her with me, so I

said yes. She ran inside, and her mother saw her packing

and asked her where she was going. She told her mother

that she was coming with me. I could hear her mother

shouting; she was upset that her daughter was still trying to

be with me. I heard her say, "Joseph's father is poor, and

Joseph is poor you need to find someone better who can do

more for you, leave Joseph alone." I will never forget

those words because a part of it was true. My father was

poor, I was poor, and I had no idea where I was going with

my life. My father didn't teach me anything. Everything I

knew I learned on my own, but I knew I loved her

daughter. I was willing to do anything to provide for her.

We went home and started our lives together after our baby. We didn't talk much about Akeem because the grief was still lingering and neither of us wanted to reopen that door.

A couple of months went by, and we got pregnant again. We were happy, and the feeling of joy was back in my life. I felt it was God blessing me again answering my prayer of being a father. We decided to be extremely careful with this pregnancy. We didn't know what went wrong with the previous pregnancy. On our first doctor's visit, we asked what went wrong, and they told us that they didn't know either. They told my girlfriend she should stay off her feet to be safe, so we did. I made sure she was well-taken care. I fed her and made sure she got her rest. I would walk with her in the mornings to the beach, then we go back home, and I would cook. I'd massage her feet and put cocoa butter lotion on her tummy. I was excited again, but a part of me still remembered the grief and pain from losing

Akeem, so I did not go over the plan. I went to work with my uncle and started to save money for the baby. Nothing changed much. I was going to be the best father in the world I could be.

One night after I got off work; I got home and went to the pipe that was about a mile from the home to get water. After I came home I was outside getting ready to take a shower I heard my girlfriend crying out for me. I ran inside, and she said she was feeling pain and she felt wet. I did not have electricity, so I grab the lamp and took a look, and there was blood all over the sheets. I started to panic so I ran to the town as fast as I could.

The first taxi I saw I told him that I thought my girlfriend was in labor and we needed to go to the hospital. We rushed to my home; where I lived was off-road we had to stop and walk the rest of the way to my house. My girlfriend was dressed and waiting for me. I could hear her crying when I reached the gate, but this cry sounded different. It didn't sound like a cry from the pain; it sounded like a cry of disappointment. It was as if she knew something was wrong. I knew that something was not right because we were only into the fifth month of the pregnancy. From the previous experience, we knew this was not normal. The taxi driver and I both carried my girlfriend to the car, we then rushed to the hospital. They immediately took her to the labor room, but unlike the last time, everything went fast. The doctor came out to see me, and the look on his face is the one I had seen before. This time I was not sad; I was mad. I was mad at everything and everyone. I kept asking how could this keep happening to me, what had I done wrong and to whom have I done it?

My girlfriend had to stay overnight for observation, so I stayed with her. If she was feeling the way I did, then neither one of us wanted to be alone. I sat by her bed and held her hand all night as we both cried together. The next day when it was time for us to go home, we packed our things and went outside. The sun was hot, and I didn't mind walking home, but with what my girlfriend had just gone through, I could not let her walk, so we took a cab home. Later that day I heard someone shouting my girlfriend's name. The voice sounded familiar; it was my girlfriend's mother. She said that she was there for her daughter and that she heard about the miscarriage. She said she had a dream that her dead great grandmother was killing the babies because my girlfriend and I are not supposed to be together.

I honestly got scared, but I still did not want to lose my girlfriend; she was all I had left. I had no choice but to let her go with her mother. It was one of the hardest things I'd ever done watching her pack right after losing my second child. In a year I felt every emotion anger, pain, love, and hate. I just wanted to give up on life at that moment. I cried as they walked through the gates.

I was still hoping to be with my girlfriend; I was hoping that was not the end of us. I would go to her neighborhood to see her, but I had to hide because her mother forbade us from being together. I would go there at night and make a noise like a dog. She would come out to the back door to see me. One night I went to see her, and she sent her cousin out to tell me that she could not make it outside that night. I was disappointed because I was hoping to see her. I went home and didn't put much thought into it, but the following night when I went back, she sent her cousin to tell me that she could not make it again. I became very suspicious because this had never happened before. I asked my girlfriend's cousin to tell me what was going on. He told me that she started seeing someone else. He was allowed to be inside the house, and that he was there inside with her right now. That was the reason she was not coming out to see me.

I was instantly heartbroken; I did not expect this. I wanted to see my girlfriend and asked her for myself. I was hurt. I went home crying in disbelief that I just lost the only person I thought loved me for good. I could not sleep; I stayed up all night waiting for morning to come so I could go back and see her. When I went to see her, I saw her with someone else laughing and being close together as I didn't exist anymore. I expected it, but I was praying it would never happen. I shouted out her name, and she looked at me standing in the street with tears running down my face. She said that her mother said that she should not be with me anymore. She said her mother said I would never amount to anything. Her words ruined my already fragile soul. That proved to me that there was not one person on the earth that I felt loved and cared for me. No one believed in me; I had no self-esteem.

All the things I'd been through molestation, abuse, losing two children in one year, and now losing the only person I thought loved me. I didn't want to continue with my life. The thought of suicide came rushing through my mind. I felt I would always be alone and no one was ever going to love me. I went home got a pen and a piece of paper and began to write my suicide letter. I wrote to my mother telling her I was sorry for not being a better son for her to love. That I loved her even though I didn't show it and that I appreciated her efforts. I wrote that I was going through a lot of pain that I couldn't live with anymore. The feeling of neglect and rejection was becoming unbearable; no one loved me, no friends, and no family.

DEPRESSION

I wrote the note and put it down, and I grabbed a knife. I went outside and saw someone's goat tied with a rope. I cut the rope with enough length to tie in the ceiling and around my neck. I went back inside and tied the knot to fit my head through, then got up on a chair and tied the rope in the ceiling. I laid on the floor for a while looking at the rope. I was looking for a reason to live, and I could not think of any, so I started to pray. I prayed continuously asking God to forgive me for what I was about to do. While I was praying, all I could think about was the hurt I was feeling. I'd never really felt love. I'd never seen love. I'd never heard the words "I LOVE YOU" from anyone. Since the age of four, I had to fight my own battles. I had so much built up inside of me, and no one was there for me.

I started to feel that it was time for me to go through with the suicide; I felt it was the moment to get up on the chair and do it. I got up and stood on the chair holding the rope around my neck getting ready to step off the chair. Out of nowhere, my mother appeared; she was not supposed to be there; she never came to visit. I was always by myself, but that day she came and saw what I was about to do. She yelled at me to stop. She started crying, she said. "Joseph I love you, if you do this you will break my heart." I stopped took the rope off from around my neck and stepped down off the chair. I could see the hurt in my mother's eyes.

The pain I saw in her eyes was what I was going through for so long. I started to cry with her; this was the first time I could remember hearing the words I love you. She hugged me so tight, and that was my first time getting embraced by anyone. After seventeen years of living, this was my first I could remember thinking that someone cared. My mother asked me what was going on, and what brought me to the point of attempting to take my life. I told her I felt as if no one loved me, that I lost everything I lost my sons, and I lost the girl I loved. I felt neglected and abandoned by everyone. She told me that she was going to move back with the family. She was going to get my brother and sisters and that we would all love together. I was hopeful even though it felt like it was too late for me because I was already ruined. I'd been living with some terrible secrets that I was too weak to share. My family was back, but living by myself for so long it still felt as if I was alone. I needed my girlfriend back. I knew money was the issue, so I figured if I get a job and bought some clothes and shoes, I'd be able to get her back. I was eighteen years old and did not own a pair of shoes or a pair of jeans. I knew I had to change that if I was ever to get my girl back.

Word got out that I attempted to commit suicide, wherever I went I could hear people talking about it, some making jokes, but I pretended not to hear. Everyone thought it was because of my ex-girlfriend and they were partly right, but it was so much I was going through my girlfriend leaving was the last straw. I made up in my mind that if I got a job, bought some shoes and some clothes, then she'd see that I was not poor anymore. I went to see my uncle about working for him again, and he said yes. I was motivated; I wanted to win my girl back. My first paycheck I went to Ocho Rios to buy some name brand clothes. I bought a pair of jeans, a shirt, a pair of Nike shoes, and my first bottle of cologne. I was excited about my new outfit.

I wanted to show it off to my now ex-girlfriend hoping to win her back. She had never seen me in new clothing before, so I thought this would make a good impression. I figured that it was time to go after her. I went to her town all dressed up smelling great, but on my way there the power went out. The entire neighborhood was in complete darkness, but I kept going. I didn't know how long the power was going to be out, but I was hoping the power would come back on by the time I got to her house. When I was almost there I felt something come over me. I paused for a minute and thought about what I was doing. I had just spent all the money I had to impress someone that did not love me anymore. I needed love, so I ignored the feeling and kept on walking.

While I was walking, I heard the sound of someone running towards me, but I figured it was someone rushing to go somewhere. I gave it no attention, but then I heard someone say, "you m***********r you." I felt a blow on my left arm; the pain was unlike any other pain I'd ever felt. By the time I could see who it was and why I was being hit the person ran off. I was about to run after the person, but then I realized that my arm was hanging off my body, and blood was spraying everywhere. I was shocked; I thought I was dreaming.

I yelled out for help, but it seemed no one could hear me. I picked up my arm and then let go, and it was hanging from my body. I then pinched myself to see if I was dreaming, but I felt the pinch, so I knew it was real.

Someone chopped me with a machete, and it went through my bones. I could not feel my fingers anymore, but losing my arm, the only thing I was thinking about was the clothing and shoes I just spent all my money to buy. My new clothing to impress my ex-girlfriend was ruined I was thinking, blood was spraying everywhere. I grabbed my left arm and held it together with my right hand and ran towards my ex-girlfriend's house.

I ran as fast as I could. I remember while running, I was thinking that there is no way this is happening to me. I ran into my ex-girlfriend's yard and yelled her name. She was sitting with her family on their front porch using candles as lights. She answered, and I yelled out to her that my arm had just been chopped off. She asked, "What?" in a confused tone. I ran up to the porch and let go of my left hand, and blood started spraying all over everyone sitting on the porch. My ex-girlfriend's mother yelled "Jesus" when she saw that my arm was hanging off my body. She told me that I should hold it back together. She told one of her daughters to get a towel and a flashlight. They put me in the middle of the street to lie down and got a piece of board. They wrapped my arm up with the towel using the board to hold it in place. I could feel the warmth of the blood running down the side of my body. It was running down so heavy it felt like someone was pouring water all over me. I was losing blood profusely, soon the news of what happened to me filled the entire neighborhood and a crowd started to gather around.

Everyone was asking what had happened. I could hear my ex-girlfriend's mother explaining that someone just chopped off my arm. I was losing too much blood; I started to go in and out of consciousness. In the midst of all that was happening, I could hear my father's voice asking who it was and what was going on. Someone said to my father, "it's your son Joseph; someone chopped off his hand." His replied, "that's what you get." The crowd started to yell at my father; they were asking him how could he say that when his son was lying here bleeding out to death on the street. My father said, "I don't care," and he walked away.

The next thing I remember was waking up in the local hospital. By the time I had reached the hospital the power had come back on. I saw the doctors and nurses running frantic trying to stop the bleeding. I looked to the right, and I saw my little sister crying begging the doctors to save my life. It was at that point that I realized the severity of the wound and I started to cry too. It hit me that I was about to die. I had been through so much. I'd never enjoyed my life, everything bad that could've happened to someone had happened to me. The doctors were able to stop the bleeding, but the wound was so severe they were unable to do anything else to assist me. They told me that they would have to transfer me immediately to a bigger hospital with better doctors and specialist. They were transferring me to Kingston Public Hospital, the biggest

hospital in Jamaica.

Before I left to go to Kingston two police officers

came in the room to speak to me. They asked if I knew

what had happened to me. I told them no, so they

explained to me that a man had turned himself in saying

that he had just chopped someone by mistake. All that had

just happened to me was because of mistaken identity. I did

not know what to think I was speechless. I figured that was

the case because I hadn't done anything wrong to anyone

neither was I in a fight. The doctor told the policemen that I

had to go right away. I was supposed to be airlifted, but

there was no helicopter available, so they had to use an

ambulance. Kingston Public Hospital was three hours

away. The doctor was writing a note to give the doctors at

the other hospital, and I asked him if he had ever seen this

type of injury before and he said no. I asked if he thought

they could save my arm and he said," I don't know" I knew he was speaking honestly at that moment.

The ride to the other hospital was long. I kept falling in and out of consciousness; every time I would wake up and see where I was I would pray. With tears filling my eyes I asked God to save me. I prayed, "Lord if there is a time I need you it is now." I don't remember reaching the hospital, but I remember waking up in pain and bandages. It was daylight, and when I opened my eyes, I saw my mother and my little sister looking down on me laying in a hospital bed. My mother told me that I had been asleep for three days; I had lost so much blood I was in a coma. I was in a lot of pain, and the pain medication was not working.

The doctors were trying to save my arm; they told my mother that normally they would finish cutting the arm off being that the bone was completely cut through. They had some young doctors that were training, and they wanted to try and save it, but they could not promise that it would work. I was optimistic, and I prayed every day that my arm would be able to be saved. I was unable to move, and my mother would travel the three hours to Kingston every day on the bus to bathe me. I was suffering from depression.

I thought nothing else could go wrong. Everything that happened to me came to me innocently. I'd never done anything wrong to anyone yet my life was horrible. I couldn't catch a break. The doctors told me that they put a metal pin through my bones and reattached the veins, and if it did not work, they would have to go ahead and cut off the arm. I was so scared, every morning the doctors and trainees would all come to my bedside to see if the arm was making progress, but it never was. They would touch my fingers and ask if I was feeling anything, and I would say no. I had no feeling at all in my left arm, but the area where the cut was in excruciating pain.

I told the doctor about the pain I was feeling. He had the nurses give me heavier pain medication that would help me to sleep. All I could think about was losing my arm, and not being the same again. I was in the wrong place at the wrong time trying to win someone's heart that never loved me. My ex-girlfriend never came to visit me the entire two months that I was in the hospital. My mother made the the trip faithfully every day, and I knew the bus fare was expensive for her. She made sure she was there as often as possible. I needed her more than ever, and I think she saw that need. I felt her love more than I'd ever felt it in my entire life. I felt the injury brought us close together.

One day while laying down on the hospital bed I had a weird feeling. I decided not to be honest the next time the doctors come around to test my fingers. I was going to tell them I could feel it even though I could not. While they were making their rounds on the floor visiting all the patients. I could see one of the doctor's looking at me. It was a look of disappointment as if the experiment they tried was not working. When they reached my bed, they poked my fingers with a needle, and I yelled out as if I was in pain. They were all surprised, the doctor did it again, and I yelled again even though I did not feel anything. He asked if I had feeling in the arm now and I told him yes. They were all excited, but they were not sure if I was telling the truth. They told me they would be back the next day and walked away.

About five minutes later I smelled the fragrance one the doctors was wearing, so I felt they were close to my bed. I was stationary in the bed so I couldn't move to see exactly where they were, but I felt their presence. I was laying down with my arm tied to a pole to keep it stable and upward so blood could flow through it. The smell of the fragrance got stronger, so I yelled again as if I felt them sticking my injured arm. They showed themselves, and one of the doctors said they were testing to make sure I had feeling in my arm. They were planning on cutting it off that very same day if it had not made any progress. I was so relieved, and even though I did not have feeling in my arm the fact that it was still there gave me hope. Every morning when they came I would continuously pretend I felt them sticking my arm. I prayed every day for feeling to come back in my arm. I would try to close my hand. In my mind, I was closing my hand, but when I looked at my fingers they were not moving.

One morning after my mother had come and bathed me, we were talking about my arm, and if I would ever be able to use my hand again. In the middle of the conversation I tried again to close my hand, and I saw my little finger move. I was so excited I told my mother to look, and she said to me that I should do it again. I did, and my little finger moved again. We both were excited and called out to the nurse. The nurse rushed over to my bed; she asked what the problem was. I showed her my little finger moving; the nurse paged the doctors to come to see. They all gathered by my bedside congratulating me on learning that my hand was working.

My mother was so happy, and even though she was laughing, I could see the tears in her eyes. I was relieved to be able to have both arms even though I knew it would never be the same again. I was in the hospital for a few more weeks before I was able to go home. In Jamaica, money was essential to live, and the only way for me to make money was being able to use both arms. I started to think about my life and what was left of it because as hard and unfair as it had been it was going to be worse. My mowther took me home after they discharged me from the hospital. She was there with me every day I thought she knew how depressed I was. I watched the world pass by me. I had to walk to the local hospital every day to have my bandages changed and my hand dressed. My hand was leaking blood every day and would carry a smell if I didn't make it to have the bandages changed. I had to pay every day to get my bandages changed. I would have to skip cleaning the wound some days because I could not afford to pay the bill.

My mother was everything to me during that time; I would have never made it without God and my mother. The fact that I was unable to use my hand made me handicap. I was unable to take showers; I was unable to use the restroom; I was unable to put my clothes on. My mother would do it all for me; as old as I was I felt like a baby. Some days I would feel like walking in the town to ease my mind off my situation. When I was in town, some people would feel sorry for me and would give me money to buy food. Others would make fun of the fact that I was only able to use one arm. They would call me "One hand" or "One hand man" and laugh at the way my hand looked. It got so bad that I started to only walk at nights when no one could see me. I remember one day, in particular, I was walking on the street and saw a young lady walking with

her sister. I said hi to her, but her sister told her that she

should not speak to me because I had a disgusting scare on

my hand. Those words were like a dagger in my heart, life,

as I knew with normal capabilities, were over. The thought

of suicide came in my mind almost every day, but my

mother made sure I was not alone.

A BIG HEART

A few months went by, and my mother and my stepfather decided to sell the home they were living in before they all moved back. It was not a lot of money, but it was enough for my mother to try and start a business. She bought a red pickup truck for my brother to driv. She wanted to buy food from the local farmers and drive into the surrounding neighborhood and sell them. That sounded like a good plan, so people would not have to leave their home to shop for food. She used some of the money to open a convenient shop for me. I was unable to do physical work only having one arm, so sitting inside the shop was perfect. All I had to do was sell what was inside the shop, and use the money from the sales I made and go back to town and buy more goods to restock the shop. That went on for a while, and business was good.

I was feeling good about myself, I was now twenty, and though I lost all capabilities in one arm, I was able to feed and clothe myself. Things started to get worse because I had a big heart I wanted to help everyone who needed assistance. When someone came to me and told me they did not have food for their kids to eat, I would take from the shop and give it to them. I would do that often; my mother would warn me that if I continued to do that, then the business would go under. I could not see someone needing to feed their children and not help. At one point in my life, I was one of those kids too, and did not think twice about helping the parents feed their children.

One night I was walking by a house that was close to mine and saw a wake, and I decided to stop. I found out it was a wake for a couple who was murdered on their. Some gunmen were running from the police and ran into their farm and saw them and kill them so that they would not leave any witnesses. I stayed to offer my condolences. I saw this young lady that turned out to be the daughter of the murdered victims. She had a baby in her arms, and she was looking sad. Tears fille her eyes. I knew that look; I could feel her pain because I was living with it for so many years. I went over to her to say hi, and we started a conversation.

A few weeks later I saw her again with her baby, and she told me that she and the baby did not have any food to eat. She said her parents used to take care of her and now they were gone so she had no one left to help her. I gave her food and told her whenever they needed anything she should come to see me. Every time I'd see her I'd ask if she was ok. I knew she had just lost both her parents; I could not relate to what she was going through, though a part of me felt like I could. I felt I'd been through the same situation because though my parents were still alive, they were none existent for most of my life. We began seeing each other more often, and I would take food from the shop for her and her baby.

One day she invited me over for dinner, and when I got there, I found out that she and her daughter were sleeping on the floor. I thought about the years I spent sleeping on the floor as a teenager, and that broke my heart. I knew first hand that was the most uncomfortable way to sleep. I was a man and knew how hard sleeping on the floor was for me, so I knew that baby and a lady must be going through hell. I decided that I was going to get a bed for both of them. I knew this guy that lived in our neighborhood that made furniture. I went to him and asked him how much it would cost to make a bed for me. He told me that he would do it for me for free because he had heard what happened to my arm and that he was sorry to hear. He said if I could manage to go in the hills and cut down the trees and bring the wood to him, he would make it no charge. I was only able to use one arm, so that was going to be a hard task.

I asked the young lady to help, and we both went into the hills and found a perfect cedar tree. I paid a guy with a chainsaw to cut it up the trees for me, so we could take it to the furniture shop for the guy to make the bed. It took about four weeks to make the bed. The young lady and I both went to the shop and took the bed back to her house. It was a long walk; we were walking through the neighborhood with the bed on our heads. I could tell that she didn't mind because she was happy she was finally able to sleep on a bed. After we put the bed in the house, I took some money from my shop to go to town to get a mattress. I knew taking that much money from the business would hurt significantly, but I felt it was for a good cause. The young lady and I went to town and got a mattress, some sheets, and pillows. We went back to her house and made her bed. It felt good inside doing good for someone that needed it. After a while, the young lady and I started dating. I felt I was in love; this felt real; we had a lot in common. We were both hurting from different things, but we were both damaged, and we were there for each other. Things were great for about three months and because I was taking so much from the shop trying to help her and others that would come seeking help. The shop started to go down pretty fast.

One day I went to see her, and I saw some guy sitting on the bed. I asked her who it was and she told me it was the baby's father. I tried to be understanding, even though I was the only one there for the baby, I figured if he is going to be there for his child, then I should support the idea. My girlfriend said to me that the baby's father wanted to spend the weekend with the baby. I told her that was ok, but I was not ok with them all sleeping together. I suggested that she stay with me. She said no and broke up with me.

I did not see that coming, how could this be happening? I gave her and her baby everything. I could not understand how I was so good to someone who could do this to me. I walked home crying. I stayed in the house for the entire weekend feeling sorry for myself. No matter what I did, or how good I was, I was unable to be truly loved. My mother kept asking me what was wrong, but every time she asked I would tell her that my arm was hurting. But that was not the truth, I was heartbroken. The following Monday morning the baby's father left and went back to his life. My ex-girlfriend sent the baby to me to ask if I was ok, I told her yes. I knew she sent the baby because she knew how protective and loving I was to kids. The things I had been through made me that way. I made sure the baby had food every day and a bed to sleep in even though I was not the baby's father.

My ex-girlfriend came to me later in the day and said she needed to speak to me. She apologized for what happened and told me that she slept with her child's father. She said that she was sorry and suggested I take her back.

All the things she was saying to me broke my heart, but I

wanted to love so bad that I agreed to give us another

chance. I tried to keep the fact that I was cheated on from

my mother, but somehow she found out. When she found

out what happened my mother told me that I should not get

back together with my girlfriend because she was using me.

She said that the reason my girlfriend slept with her baby's

father and broke up with was that her baby's father looked

as if he had money. I did not listen; I did not want to hear

that because I was in love with my girlfriend. My mother

was furious that I was not willing to let go of the

relationship with my girlfriend. I had to move out and live

in with girlfriend so we could be together. The house was a

one-room shack, but we were together, and I was happy. I

felt like I belonged to something. I was a provider and a

protector to my little family. The convenient shop that I

owned was going down rapidly. I was using it to feed my

now family, so I was unable to keep it going. I was

running out of money fast.

One night my girlfriend told me that she was going

to a party with her friends. I did not want to do anything

that night, so I went to sleep. The next morning, I woke up

after hearing a familiar voice call my name. I looked

beside me and realized that my girlfriend had not made it

home yet=. The person that was calling me was the

boyfriend of my girlfriend's friend. He was calling me to

find out if my girlfriend had come home. I told him no. He

told me that his girlfriend did not come home either. I

started to worry because I knew my girlfriend had lost her

parents to violence. I prayed that she was ok. The guy and

I walked and asked everyone we saw if they had seen two

young girls and described what they were wearing. We

finally found someone that had seen them, and they told us

that they saw them checking into a motel in town with two

men. I could not believe that this was happening again. The

other guy was mad, he was threatening to hurt his

girlfriend, but all I could think about was what my mother

had me.

I wanted to tell my mother what I was going

through, but I could not stand to hear, "I told you so." The

guy and I waited until both girls got home. We already

knew where they were, but they came home and told us that

they fell asleep at some friend's house. We knew they were

lying, so we told them what we heard, and they confessed.

My girlfriend cried to me and begged me not to leave. She

said the guy she spent the night with was a soldier. She said

he told her he wanted her. She thought they were going to

be together, but she made a mistake. She asked me to

forgive her, and that said she would never do it again. I told

her that she had done this before, and also promised not to

do it again. In the middle of our argument, she told me I

should get her pregnant. She said if I were to get her

pregnant she would never cheat again and we would be a

complete family. I believed her; she knew that all I ever wanted was a family of my own, so we got pregnant. The idea of a family was fulfilling to me; It became my purpose.

The small business I had gone bankrupt. I was using the money to help everyone who I thought needed help and feeding my family and not putting money back in the business. I was broke with no source of income. I was only able to use one arm, and most jobs required the use of both arms. It became hard, and I was begging my mother for food to feed my family. I would go in the morning for breakfast and in the evening for dinner and take enough home to feed my girlfriend and her child. Although my mother never approved of the relationship she was helping me because she knew I was unable to work because of my injury.

A month later, my girlfriend was pregnant with my child; I worried a lot about how I was going to be able to take care of my family. I had to find a job I could do where

being able to use one arm would be acceptable. I couldn't

find a job, so I went to my uncle that was a contractor. He

gave me a job, but I was unable to do much as a laborer. I

knew he was helping me out the best he could because of

my situation. There were days when just lifting my arm

was painful. The bones in my arm were pinned together,

and I could feel the metal inside my arms moving.

Sometimes just standing with my hands by my side felt as

if I was lifting something heavy, it was a constant struggle.

I knew no other way; there was no easy job on the

construction site. I did my best every day.

My girlfriend and I lived in a one-room shack that

her parents left when they died. My girlfriend's brother

wanted it; her family figured since she was having my baby

that I had to find a place for her to live. While working at

the construction site, I would wait until night to take the

leftover boards when my uncle was finished working. I

gathered as much as I could before the job ended. The job

lasted for two months. I knew it was stealing and if I got

caught, I would be out of a job or probably get arrested.

When the job was finally over, we had some money saved.

I decided to go ahead use the boards I had stolen to make a

house for my family. I went into the hills to cut trees down

with my machete to use them to make the frame of the

house. I was doing this with no help, and no idea of what I

was doing. Being homeless was the only other option. I

could not let my child be born without somewhere to live,

so that was all the motivation I needed. I had no help

making the frame of the house, and it was hard putting

everything all together. There were times I would walk

around and look at the unfinished houses around me and try

my best to copy what I saw. The door and windows were

extremely important to get right.

It took me about one month to finish the house. It

was so small I could only fit a queen size bed inside, and a little makeshift table I made with some of the remaining boards. I was finally in my own home that I made with one hand though it was not made well. I could stay inside and see outside through the holes in the walls because they weren't put together well. The roof of the house had so many holes in it that when it rained, there was water everywhere. I use to pray that it didn't rain because when it did the bed would get wet. We would have to take the mattress out to lay in the sun when the rain stopped.

ANDRE

I 20 years old and still searching for a job. I had no shoes, but I decided that would not stop me. I went into town and stopped at every business place to inquire about available jobs. I let them know that I was only able to use one arm. Most of the business places needed physical laborers to load and unload trucks, so I was unsuccessful. I felt hopeless, but I kept going. I went to the local bakery in town. I went inside and asked to speak with a manager. The owner came out to speak to me, she asked, "what can I do for you, sir?" I replied, "mam, I have a pregnant girlfriend and child at home, and we are without food. Is there any way I could get a job here please?" She asked what could I do as far as baking. I told her not much, but I figured I could put the bread and pastries in bags with one arm. The manager told me that they did not have any positions open at that time as far as in the bakery, but hearing my story, she would see what she could do.

She went inside for a while then came back out and asked if I could use a broom with my one arm. I told her I was not sure, but I would learn. She told me to come back the next morning, and she would show me what to do. I was excited I could not wait to get home and tell my girlfriend that I finally had a job. When I got home, I told her the news, and she was happy. The next day I went to work, and I had to be on the outside to clean around the building because I had no shoes. It was unsafe and unsanitary to be inside with no shoe. I was at work every day and with my first paycheck I went and bought a pair of cheap shoes. I gave my girlfriend the rest of the money to buy groceries. I was finally able to do more than just clean outside the bakery. I was allowed to clean inside the bakery because I had on shoes. I would watch what the bakers were doing; I wanted to learn because I was getting just the base pay and though I was grateful I wanted to make more money. I wanted to make a better home for my unborn child. We saved some money, and I went to Kingston where baby clothing was cheaper if you buy in bulk. I went and got as much clothing as I could, but it was not much. I was proud that I was able to be prepared for my child coming. My girlfriend did not like our living conditions and used to complain a lot. She was not happy, she wanted more, but I needed her.

I was much more prepared for this child after learning from the past two pregnancies with my ex-girlfriend. I made sure I had a taxi prepared. I took the taxi driver's number and told him that I would call him at any time, and let him know to be prepared for my call. I did not care how much it cost to get my girlfriend to the hospital.

One early Wednesday morning in 2004 my girlfriend was crying out in pain as if she was about to go in labor. I called the taxi driver I had planned to take us and grabbed the bag of clothing that was packed and prepared for the hospital. When we get there, they immediately took her back to the labor room. I was so

worried and scared I could not stand still. I was pacing up

and down the hall just waiting for someone to come and tell

me that the baby was ok. I chose not to know the sex of the

baby while my girlfriend was pregnant. I had the feeling

something would go wrong like it always did so I did not

pick out a name. I was willing to be grateful for a child no

matter what the sex.

I heard the crying in the delivery room, and my

heart filled with joy. I knew that was the cry of my child. I

could not wait to hold him or her in my arm. I was finally

allowed to see my baby, and they told me it was a boy. I

was so happy an angel was born. He was my savior. He

instantly became the most meaningful, loving thing in my

life. I would rush home from work every day to be with my

baby; I could never put him down. Life was still hard trying

to make ends meet, but my son (Andre) gave me hope. My

girlfriend was still unhappy, and we would argue about money.

She had a friend that was with a guy who had a better job making more money. Her friend would brag about the things he was able to do for her. At some point, my girlfriend's friend told her about some other guy that she knew that had money. He was single, so my girlfriend decided to break up with me to be with him. One day I came home from work and saw my girlfriend packing her stuff to leave. I was beside myself; she was taking everything I ever needed. Everything she promised I would have for the rest of my life. Everything I ever dreamed about. I could not give her much financially, but I loved her with everything in me. I wanted my own family that I could provide for, love, and protect. I was crying to her begging her not to go with tears running down my face she said to me, "I have to go; my friend is outside waiting for me."

Her friend was outside waiting to help her carry her stuff to the bus stop.

I watched her walk away with her child walking and my baby in her arms until they were out of sight. I could not stop crying; everyone I loved was walking out of my life. I did not know where they were going, and I had no clue if I was ever going to see them again. I needed more money or a better job to get my family back. I started thinking about what I needed to do because I could not make it through a day without crying. I prayed every night and every day that my girlfriend would come back and we could be a family again.

About three weeks later I saw her and the baby and my heart stopped. She was walking in the path towards my house with bags in her hand. I thanked God for answering my prayers for letting her come back with my son. I was happy and I ran to meet her. When I got to her I was smiling from ear to ear; I did not care about what she did or where she was I was just happy to see my family. She said to me "I am only here to drop your son off." I asked her, "What do you mean?" She told me that the guy she was with did not want a young baby around because they make too much noise. She had to take the baby back to me. I was speechless. I didn't know what to say to her. I could not believe what was happening. I told her that it would be impossible for me to work with the baby because I didn't have any help to care for the baby while I went to work. Andre was only three months old. She left after I told her that I could not take Andre.

As I was up thinking about our conversatio I heard a knock on the door. I asked who it was, but there was no answer, so I opened the door. When I looked down my son was laying there in the dark wrapped up on the ground. His mother had knocked on my door and put him there for me to see then ran off. I called out her name, but I heard no answer; she was not ther. I quickly picked him up off the ground and took him inside. I cried with him in my arms, that night I stayed up all night I only had the bottle she left with him for food. I had no idea what to do; I thought it was all a dream; there was no way all this was happening. I was used to everyone walking out of my life, but now my three-month-old son is a part of the life that I hated. I promised my son that night that I would never leave him no matter what happened. I got up early the next morning for work. I had no one to care for my son, so I took him to work with me. I went straight into the owner of the bakery's office and explained my situation that I was in suddenly. She understood and said she would give me a couple of days off to figure out what to do.

I didn't know how to change a diaper. I was clueless about how to take care of a baby. That week I got paid and went to a store in town and bought the cheapest stroller I could find. I also bought baby food and baby clothing. Life was just Andre and me. I went to work the next Monday because I could not miss any more days. I still had no help, so I took Andre with me in the stroller I bought over the weekend. I went into the owner's office letting her know that I needed the job, but I had no one to care for my baby while I worked. She felt sorry for me and told me that I could put the baby in the stroller around the back. I would periodically check on him while I worked. I was grateful for her being considerate to my situation. Without a job with the baby, would have been impossible.

The owner of the bakery had a son that would come to the bakery from time to time. He was not fond of the idea of me working there with a baby inside the building. He would ask his mother why not just let me go since it was so complicated for me to do my job. It was not safe for the baby, and that was understandable to me, but I had no choice. His mother explained to him what happened and even though he did not agree, his mother had the final say. I was able to remain employed. A couple of months later the owner of the bakery went on vacation. She left her son to fill in for her while she was out. I had no idea that she was leaving, so when I got to work and saw the son in the office, I was surprised. The first thing he did when he saw me was call me in the office. He said to me that he was going to have to let me go because of my baby situation. He said that we were bad for business. I busted out in tears right in front of him; I begged him not to do it because I didn't know what to do. I had no one else to turn to, but he told me that he also had no choice in the matter. I walked out of the office pushing the stroller with Andre in it. I was still crying, but when I looked down on Andre, he was smiling. He had no clue what I was going through. I was now out of a job with no help and wouldn't be able to provide for my child. After walking out of the bakery, I stood on the side of the street thinking about what I should do next.

There was a ministry of labor building right next to the bakery, and I decided to go over there. I wanted to talk to someone to see if what happened to me was legal. I spoke with a representative about what had just happened. I asked if they could fire me from a job like that without doing anything wrong. I explained to her my situation of not having care for my son, and that I was a single father. I had to take my son with me every day to work. I also told her that the owner of the bakery said it was ok for me to work there and that she was on vacation, and the son that was filling in for did not approve of me working at the bakery with my son, so he fired me. They informed me that they were unable to get me my job back, but they can see that I get two weeks' pay. I was excited when they told me this because I would now be able to provide for my son for the next two weeks.

I went home with the baby without a clue on what to do next. I had bread and cake at home that I would take from the bakery at nights. That was what I ate for my breakfast and dinner; I bought milk for Andre. I tried to make the two weeks' pay last as long as possible. The injury to my arm and having a young baby made it harder finding a job to accommodate me. I found out the owner of the bakery was back from vacation so I figured I would try to get my job back. The owner of the bakery said it was too late that she was unable to undo what her son had done. She said it would be disrespectful to him being that he is part owner of the business. It was hard for me.

I kept praying every day and asked God why is my life like this. I felt beaten up and cast aside as if I was left to die, but I kept fighting to stay alive for my son. I felt like he needed me, and he did because it was just us. It looked like everyone was enjoying their lives and I was going through the worst experiences. I would stay in bed late because I did not want to get up and use my energy. I knew whatever food and money I had were to last us because when it was gone I had nowhere to go for help. I used to put Andre on my chest to fall asleep at night that was the only way he would sleep. We became attached to each other, spending every minute of every day together. Everywhere I went I had the stroller pushing along.

The money and food finally ran out. I had to figure out how to get by so I started breaking into my uncle's house. He was the contractor that used to hire me to work. He had a son too that was my Andre's age, so when I broke into his place, I would go directly for the baby's food. I'd take enough home to last my son through the day but not enough for it to seem noticeable. I tried to be careful not to let it be noticeable that someone was taking from it. I would also look for things for myself to eat, and sometimes I couldn't find anything. When that happened, I would go through the day without food. I was happy to know that Andre had food to eat and was not hungry. I sometimes would try to force him to sleep during the day time. I'd try to sleep then because if I were up, I would be hungry and weak.

One day I remembered going to my brother's place and told him that my son and I were hungry. I asked if he had anything to eat or any money I could have to buy something to eat. He said he had nothing either. It was hard on everyone, so I believed him, but I looked on his dresser and saw a twenty dollar coin which would be enough to get milk for my son. I asked my brother if I could have the twenty dollar coin and he said he was going to use it. I left and went home, but something inside me said I should go back over to my brother's place. When he left, I went back to his place and looked through his window. I was able to see on top of his dresser, and the twenty dollar coin was still there. I broke into his house through the window and took the twenty dollars. I closed the window and left his place just as it was before I broke in. The only thing I needed was milk for my son because he was hungry and twenty dollars was enough. I went to the store and got the milk and fed my son. I was still hungry, but my son was not, and that meant everything to me. I was laying down listening for my brother to come and ask me for the twenty dollars. I stayed up late waiting, but he never came.

The next day I went over to his place I had guilt all over my face. I was going to admit taking the money if he asked me, but he didn't. I realized that my brother did not miss the money. He did not need it as I thought he did, that broke my heart. It hurt to know that my brother knew that I had no food for my baby, his nephew, and if he could afford to get him something to eat why say no. I couldn't understand it, until this day I never said anything to my brother about taking the money. I used that as confirmation that it was just my son and I against the world. We had no one else to turn to for anything.

One night I was lying in bed with Andre laying on my chest, I had just fed him the last of the milk I had. I was up thinking of where I would get something for him. I woke up early the next morning before the baby and left him asleep. I wanted to go search for something for him to eat before he woke up. I was going to my uncle's place more often because I had no other choice, but it seemed as if he knew someone was breaking in his home. The window I normally would go through had extra bolts on them. I decided I had to get in I could not go back home with anything for Andre to eat when he woke up. It took a while, but I was finally able to get inside.

As I was collecting food for Andre, I suddenly felt a weird feeling. It was as if something was wrong with Andre. I had left him at home in bed by himself. The bond we had from being together all day every day was so strong I could sense something was not right. I grabbed all that I could and went back through the window of my uncle's house. I ran as fast as I could trying to get home. I was almost home when I saw a group of people standing next to my house. When I reached our house I saw Andre standing there crying and the people standing there asking him where I was. He had crawled outside looking for me after he had woken up and did not see me. He was little he could not understand what they were saying to him. I pushed through the crowd and picked him up and held him tight in my arms and said to him. "Daddy is here. I will never leave you again I promise." I took him inside and fed him the milk I had taken from my uncle.

Andre was now ten months old and would crawl and stand up for a little then fall. He had trouble standing straight, since I was only able to use one arm I kept him in the stroller more than I should. His back curved to the shape of the stroller. I was worried that he might not be able to walk. An old lady saw me with Andre one day and saw that his back was curved. She told me to take Andre to the beach every day and plant him waist deep in the sand. She said I should put him where the waves would wash up and have the sand form firmly around him. I took Andre to the beach every day for two months. I would wake up early in the morning and take Andre to the beach to plant him waist deep in the sand and watch the waves wash up on him. I would pray that it worked and that he would be able to walk. I started noticing the difference over time; his back started looking more and more straightened. He started making steps. The day he made his first step I was so happy I ran to the old lady's home that gave me the advice and thanked her. She saved my son. I could not thank her enough.

I was still having a hard time providing food for Andre and breaking into houses. Begging was becoming so overwhelming for me. At the time my mother was worked as a housekeeper for a lady that lived in Ocho Rios, so I hardly saw her. One day she came to town, and we talked.

I told her I did not know what to do. Life was becoming unbearable. I was doing my best to provide for my son, but it was not enough. She told me that the lady she worked for was the manager of a hotel in Ocho Rios. She said she would talk to her about a job for me. My mother went back to work and spoke to the lady. She called my brother and told him to let me know that the lady had got me an interview. I had no shoes or clothes to wear to the interview, but I knew I had to go. I could not miss that opportunity of finally being able to provide food for my son.

My brother had a pair of shoes and a shirt, and we both wore the same size. The day before the interview I went over to his house and begged him to let me wear his clothes and shoes to the interview. I was tired of the life I was living breaking into homes and begging for food to feed my child. This opportunity would change our I lives for the better. My brother said yes, and he gave me the clothes and shoes. The idea of having a job was exciting. I was filled with optimism, but I needed someone to take care of Andre while I went to the interview. My older sister had three kids, and their father was out of a job also. Life was hard for them too. I went to her and promised her that if she watched over Andre while I went to the interview and if I got the job, I would pay her to watch Andre.

She was fond of the idea because it would be a source of income for her, so we made a deal. I was excited about going to bed thinking of the possibilities of finally getting a job. The things I could do for my son. I woke up the next morning feeling nervous. It had dawned on me that I had no experience in the hotel industry and I was only able to use one arm. I figured I would go anyway; I got dressed then I went to see my brother for cab fare that he promised to loan me. I prayed the whole way to the interview begging God please to help me get this job.

When I reached the hotel for the interview, I was sent to a hall. When I got to the hall, it was filled with people who were also there for an interview. Most of them were from other hotels or graduating from hotel schools where they learned hotel skills. Everyone had experience and/or were certified. In my mind, I thought I was never going to get the job. Everyone that went into the interview had a smile on their face coming out.

It was finally my time to be interviewed. The man conducting the interview had a piece of paper with my name on it. I shook his hand and sat down; he then said, "Joseph, tell me about you," I said, " well, sir I am twenty-two years old with a one year child at home. I am a single parent because my son's mother left when he was only three months old to be with someone else, so getting this job would be my only source of income. I have been doing it all by myself, and frankly, I don't know how I'm able to." He said, "Ok, impressive now what kind of skills do you have and how would you be an asset to this hotel?" I said, "I have never worked in a hotel before or went to school to do so, but I am a very motivated man. I will be here every day on time. My only experiences are from construction work and cleaning a bakery. I am dedicated to providing for my son, so I will be dedicated to giving this establishment my one hundred percent at all times." He said to me, "Ok, then I will see you here on Monday at nine am for orientation." He did not tell me what I would be doing, but I was so happy I didn't remember to ask. It didn't matter because working at a hotel was almost everyone's dream from my neighborhood. I could wait to get home to tell my brother and sister.

The first day of the new job I got up super early and took Andre to my sister's and went to work. I was there at eight thirty am. I found out then that I was in the housekeeping department because of my inexperience and inability to do much with just one arm. I was on the

graveyard shift where I would work from eleven pm at
night to seven the next morning. My job was to clean the
restrooms and give extra towels or sheets to the guest if
they should ever need them. I wasn't used to being up all
night, but the shift worked out great because Andre was
asleep while I worked. When I get home, we would get to
spend the day together. The hotel provided me with
uniforms, and they had a bus for the employees that rn
before every shift. I had clothes to wear and a reliable ride
to work. I was happy I was able to provide food for my
son, pay my sister to care for him while I go to work, and
buy clothes and shoes for him.

After a month of working with my pay plus tips, I
was able to buy my first television. It was a twenty-inch
TV. I was happy my life was finally ok for once. The
month after that I bought a radio. I was now able to do
things for my son and myself that I was not able to do
before. Andre's mother came into town about six months

after I started working and things were a lot better than when she left. She had broken up with the guy she left to be with, and she wanted to come back. The pain in my heart would not allow me to take her back. I wanted to forgive her, but I just could not. When I needed her the most, she walked out and left my son and I. Even though I loved her I could not get over the fact that she left. I had a good job, and Andre was older walking and talking. I could not let anyone in our lives that would leave us. I did not trust anyone even if they promised they would stay. She begged for my forgiveness, but I could not forgive her.

We had sex a few times when she would visit, but that was it. I knew she was only coming around because I was doing better. Andre and I were by ourselves when we were doing bad, and no one was there for us. I chose for us to be by ourselves when we started doing better. All the things I had been through made me overprotective of my son. I didn't want anyone to abandon, neglect, abuse, or molest him as I was and I kept him away from everyone, even his mother. Life was not perfect, but it was better than it was before. Taking care of my son was all that was important to me. I made my life completely about him. Every decision I made had thoughts about him and how whatever I was doing would it impact him.

TO BE CONTINUED.

ACKNOWLEDGMENTS

It became a dream of mine to write a book. I grew older and started to have a love for writing. My life was filled with distractions. I could never stay focused long enough to do anything constructive. I was always with the wrong crowd, in the clubs spending money I didn't have and trying to impress people that never cared about me. I was spending time away from my son and not fulfilling my potential as a father, breaking the promises I made to my mother.

I first want to thank Keera. She was the first person I felt believed in me. I remember walking in the store together to buy pens and note pads. If it weren't for you, I would never start writing. You brought stabil,ity to my life. April, your energy was amazing to me. That conversation we had was the most important one. I told you I wanted to write, and you asked me what I waiting on was, but in my mind, I was thinking a perfect time. You made me realize that the time was now. Katrinia, your attention to detail and your unfiltered opinions were very important. Your proofreading of this book was great. The phone calls you made; the emails you sent was amazing work. You are a true friend. Nisa, you are a very smart young lady. Your intelligence is superior to a lot of people; you helping to edit and proofread this book was one of my best decisions. Antorine, I want to say thank you from the bottom of my heart. There were so many times you were there for me when I had nowhere else to go. You are a real friend. Omar Clarke, you are my little brother, but I look up to you in so many ways. When I was lost you were taking care of mom, and that was something great because I could not find myself. I love you brother.

54820079R00114

Made in the USA
Columbia, SC
08 April 2019